A POET,
A LIFE

A POET,
A LIFE

A Celebration
of the Complexities of Life

Martha Baskin

To order additional copies of this book, contact:
Xlibris
844-714-8691
www.Xlibris.com
Orders@Xlibris.com
840584

CONTENTS

WRITING

FAMILY AND FRIENDSHIP

WANDERINGS

THE MANY OTHERS IN OUR LIVES

THE SERENDIPITY OF JOY

EXISTENTIAL PONDERINGS

DEATH AND MOURNING

LOVERS, LOVE, AND ITS COMPLEXITIES

STORIES

Writing

To all the men I've loved—especially
my father Fay, my brother John, my
husband Jack, and my son Hank

Iambic Pentameter

**(Why I Switched from Prose to Poetry in Miss
Regina's Eleventh Grade English Class)**

Miss Regina Pinkston was born in 1901, the year Queen *Victoria
Regina* died, and named in her honor. When she taught me English
during my junior year at Manchester High School, she was as regal
as any queen and treated her students with gentleness and grace. She
lived in a large, white, two-story antebellum house with a wraparound
porch in the neighboring town of Greenville, and except for going
to boarding school in nearby Atlanta, she had never left that western
corner of Georgia. Miss Regina was warm and loving, always willing
to listen to stories of what was going on in our lives and compare our
world to the one she had lived in as a girl.

When America entered the Great War in April of 1917, Miss
Regina had been our age and in her senior year at one of Georgia's
best finishing schools. She often told us that she always felt that from
that April day on, the world would never be the same. When she
spoke of that spring, her expression softened even further, became
wistful, and her voice dropped almost to a whisper. She shook her
head back and forth a few times and said, "No, sir, we would never
be unselfconscious again. What we lost, as a country and as a people,
was our innocence." After a pause and a faraway look in her eyes,
she said, "At commencement that spring, it wasn't just our class that
was commencing a new life, but the whole world."

Miss Regina never married. She wasn't what we considered
a *single lady* like the Math teacher who dated Ernest Bowman's
widowed father and went dancing with him at the Moose Club, or a
spinster like the librarian who always wore a cameo on her lapel and
old lady lace-up shoes that smelled of shoe polish. She was simply
girlishly unattached. We knew that she took care of her elderly father,
but nothing else was ever mentioned. To us, she was as mysterious
a figure as Emily Dickinson only not as reclusive. We speculated

among ourselves that since she often talked about the Great War, she might have had a beau she loved very much who was killed in battle.

It was in Miss Regina's orderly, kind, and gentle world I learned that, in America, the fog always comes up on little cat's feet, it is preferable to take the road less traveled, good fences make good neighbors, and someone named Richard Cory is a good example of not being able to tell from outward appearances what someone's life is really like.

She introduced me to rhymes. When I had trouble with pronouncing words or remembering their meaning, she provided me with a rhyming word. "Bounce those two around, now," she told me. "And it will be easier for you to remember. It's the Scot in me, you see," she said with a wink. "You get two for the price of one." Diphthongs, as pronounced in *Jaw-Jah* (Georgia), were particularly troublesome and the silent letters in words like *bot* (bought) and *thot* (thought) seemed so much easier to remember when I tackled them in pairs.

I needed a little extra help from Miss Regina because English was not my native language. I had moved to the United States from South America the year before, and words still sounded strange in English, but I loved the way they looked on the page and read voraciously. I read as if I were using Spanish phonemes and pronounced every letter except the letter *H*, for that letter is always silent in Spanish. Sometimes this habit made me stare at a word and struggle to understand how words could change so much from visual to auditory rendition. *Oh-oo-say* became *house*. *Hahm* became *Jam, troh-oo-blay* became *trouble*, which is what I was usually in when my turn came to read out loud in class.

My slips of the tongue and mispronunciations soon became a source of good-natured teasing and laughter. I tried to accept that Southerners laugh at people only when they approve of them, but it was difficult because where I had grown up that sort of laughter was considered an affront to a person's dignity. I was a true oddity in school, the only non-Georgia native, a *foreigner,* and treated with deference and good humor by the staff and classmates. Although I didn't always understand the nuances of my new life, I desperately wanted to belong, but I felt excluded by my use of language.

My bridge, my private time between school and family, was the twenty-minute walk home through tree line streets appropriately named Elm and Oak, to the parsonage at 5 Maple Street. It was then when I was alone and no one could see or hear me, that I played the game I devised to improve my English. I imagined writing a word on a blackboard. Instead of reading it using Spanish phonemes, I tried to say it out loud correctly. As I walked, I skipped and chanted, intrigued by the *ta-tum ta-tum ta-tum* iambic cadence of the English language which was in such a contrast to my native language's syncopated rhythm. As I read the words on my imaginary blackboard, I was careful to pronounce them using American English rhythm.

That year, I was sixteen years old, ready to begin life. But unlike most of my classmates who were unselfconsciously involved in thinking about proms, boyfriends, and borrowing Dad's keys to go for a malt at the "Shack," I was walking home from school as if I were skirting the edge of a fjord. On one side stood a tall unscalable mountain, the country I had left behind, and to which I would never return. On that mountain, I had left my memories, my history, my vision of the future, my laughter, and my song. My heroes were there, my national holidays, as well as the southern hemisphere stars and seasons. On the other side of the fjord was an equally tall mountain, the country in which I would now live forever. On that mountain, I knew I would find new seasons, new stars, new red-letter days, new rhythms, and new songs. But I was walking on the edge of a river, a deep sinuous river which I had to navigate and then cross to attempt to climb the mountain. The river was the flow of the English language.

To Miss Regina's credit, she had the wisdom to allow me to daydream. When English language overload became numbing, she no longer looked my way or called on me. "Sometimes you need benign neglect," she explained and tacitly allowed me the liberty to remove myself temporarily from the goings-on of the class. Absentmindedly, I doodled and scribbled on the margins of my notebook. It was in that tuned-out trance state that I started experimenting with English rhymes and soon began to mimic the poets we studied. One day, Miss Regina walked by my desk, looked down at what I had written, patted me on the back, and said, "Not bad. A little like Robert Frost. Keep it up!"

Under her tutelage, my soul, not my heart, burst with lyric enthusiasm. It was still difficult for me to conceptualize the heart as being the center of emotion. My *alma* was where I felt emotion. My soul, which was certainly a *part* of me, but not part of my body. *The heart*, I thought, *is another strange American notion; one does not love or feel with a heart.* A heart is an organ, just as any other! What happens if one suffers from a faulty heart like my cousin who had rheumatic fever as a child? Would having an impaired heart impair feeling? *No*, I thought, *it is best to keep on feeling with the soul.*

My soul, accustomed to a treeless expanse of grass bordered by mighty rivers was becoming acclimated to a landscape that was markedly different and was moved with emotion as it explored the winding streams cutting through the red Georgia clay and the forests of green rolling through fog bottoms. My soul, or at least some reaches of my soul, was becoming Americanized. My soul sang, and when it sang, it sang in English, *ta-tum, ta-tum, ta-tum.*

One day, busy daydreaming, I had turned my desk a little with my back turned to the class and was looking out the window. Suddenly, the holly bushes around the flagpole caught my eye. They glistened. They glistened with a fine coat of snow, snow falling quietly and imperceptibly. *Snow! "Nieve!"* I blurted out, rising a little from my desk, toward the class. "S-s-s-noh!" I stammered and pointed out the window. By then, snow was falling in large flakes which melted as they hit the ground. Some of them stuck to the windowpanes and lingered there. Soon the panes were covered with snowflakes. As we crowded by the windows, staring at the snowfall, which was such an uncommon event in Georgia, Miss Regina took a magnifying glass out of her drawer and walked over to us. "Before we resume our work, let's look at the snowflakes on the windowpanes through this," she said. "You see, each of them is different."

How rich was my life, I thought. It was flanked by both memory and discovery. Yet somehow, I felt very much alone despite my affection for Miss Regina and my new friends. They were not acquainted with what I had left. They didn't know about our mighty, wide rivers, nor the great *pampas,* nor about our flag which was like the sky, pale blue and white with a huge yellow sun in its center. They didn't know the stories of Martin Fierro or how much we venerated all those men who had struggled and fought for our independence from Spain. They didn't know about my schoolmates María, Tita, and Beatriz, and our boyfriends who waited for us after class at the *plaza* and carried our books to the bus stop.

And I was beginning to discover America, the real America, not the one I had read about in books. America was green, America was Protestant, America ate popcorn at the movies. There were hit parades, fourth of July parades, and homecoming parades. There was Washington, Jefferson, and Mickey Mantle.

I understood the world I'd left behind. I understood the undulating roll of the land, the wind that blew strong and refreshing bringing with it the sweet smell of the *pampas.* In the region where I had grown up, we had no snow, we had no forests and streams, only endless fields of flax and wheat and wide uncrossable rivers. My world was the melancholy world of the *gaucho,* of Evita Perón, of the Southern Cross. I wanted my classmates and Miss Regina to understand it too as I was beginning to understand their world. But how could I tell them about it?

As the first term came to an end, Miss Regina announced, "I would like for everyone to write a story. It will be a contest, really. To make the judging fair, the stories should all be about the same subject. What I would like for you to write about is some sort of craftsman."

Where I had grown up, we had flat-roofed, stucco houses. As houses went up, scaffolds were placed around them and the plaster was laboriously raised in buckets by an *albañil,* a plasterer. I loved to watch the plasterers work as they raised and lowered their buckets. I admired their skill and their craftsmanship. They were poor, but they worked hard. Their hands were blistered by the lye in the plaster and cut by the ropes used to raise and lower the buckets. I wanted to write a story about an *albañil*, about his hands giving evidence of his labor.

I didn't know how to say *plasterer* so I wrote a story about *housebuilders*. I had never seen a house being built in the United States, so I did not know that plasterers did not mix the lye, sand, and water and transport it in buckets to the scaffolds.

After I wrote my story, I practiced reading it aloud in front of a mirror just as Miss Regina had suggested. I marked all the *h*'s so that I would not forget to pronounce them and even scanned the text, as I would a poem. Iambic prose: *ta-tum, ta-tum, ta-tum.*

The moment came. My turn to read my story. I stood by my desk and read out loud with a resolute voice, full of pride and confidence in my correct pronunciation. As I read, Miss Regina placed her elbows on her desktop forming a little tripod for her chin which rested on her folded hands. Her eyes never left my face. Soon, her expectant smile faded, and a puzzled look met my eyes. I glanced around the room at my classmates and noticed the same puzzled look. Charlie, the class cut-up began to snigger derisively. With a faltering voice, I concluded my story and waited for Miss Regina's assessment which fell on me like blinding light.

"The story is nicely written, but it makes no sense at all. I've never seen a builder with red hands. Builders don't have red hands."

Tears of embarrassment and frustration welled in my eyes. I could *see* the plasterer's red, raw hands. I knew the *albañil* had red hands. Why didn't Miss Regina?

My parents were Southern Baptists who were both very idealistic and generous. They met during college, and it was there that they were also "called" to the mission field by their strong desire to serve humanity. War was about to break, and posts were scarce. China, Africa, and the Middle East were closed to American missionaries, so they were sent to South America instead. The bustling, sophisticated metropolis of Buenos Aires was not exactly what they had envisioned for themselves as a "field" nor were the fields of wheat that extended endlessly in all directions in the nearby *pampas*. It was there, in Buenos Aires, that I was born, four days before the Japanese bombed Pearl Harbor.

In the late 50s, we returned to what my parents considered "reality" and my father took the post of a Baptist Church pastor in the small Georgia town of Manchester.

It was in this small town in Georgia where I now stood, trembling from head to foot clutching the pages of my story and feeling, not seeing, Miss Regina smiling gently and encouragingly. True, my parents were Americans, but was I? I had been born in a Catholic country, under the light of the Southern Cross, with the wind of the pampas cooling hot, humid December days, and the sweet, melancholy strains of the *tango* music echoing in the *barrios*. Who was I? How could I share my memories with my American friends?

The next day began a new grading period, one in which we would concentrate on poetry instead of fiction. "I've chosen Walt Whitman as our first poet," said Miss Regina, "I think you will enjoy 'Song of Myself.' Not only is the poet singing about himself, but he is also telling us about his world. I might add," she went on, "that if any of you want to write a poem for extra credit, you may. It doesn't have to be in Whitman's style, but do write about yourselves."

Ah, there was my chance, I thought. Maybe I could even pull my grade up. My sister had recently given me a copy of *A Shropshire Lad,* by A. E. Housman, and I had written a couple of poems copying his style. *By writing in song,* I thought, *I could write about all the fantastic realities of my life, and no one could question their veracity*! With song, I could tell them, and they would understand all about my father of Irish descent who took his family to a faraway land where his children grew and flourished in golden fields of wheat, and so I wrote:

My father was a Leprechaun,
My mother was the wind,
My birthplace was a far-off place
Away from help of friend.

The muses, they abducted me
When I was four days old,
And made of me a prisoner
In castles made of gold.

And I grew up in loneliness
In my captivity,
And in my melancholy world,
Knew not reality.

And now away from golden fields,
Away from guardian Muse,
I'll sing my melancholy songs
And put them all to use.

When Miss Regina read my poem she smiled and said, "Looks like reading *A Shropshire Lad* really made an impression on you. You'll love the British literature we will study next year in the twelfth grade. Try writing some sonnets over the summer. Should be easy for you. Study Shakespeare's form, and remember," she added with a wink, "iambic pentameter!"

Ortigas (Nettles)

I became a writer when words were all I had to
reconstruct the nettles, the brown water of the river,
the roaring wind that knocked me over in its springtime fury.

All that was lost. All that disappeared in the leaving.
My parents came North, taking me with them—
memory, they left behind.

They said, *Hurry! No time to lose!*
We must pack! We must go!
Take only what you can carry!

Nettles were a nuisance to me, clinging to my clothes,
cutting my skin, making small spidery scratches.
And the river, how it sullied our bodies with fine gray residue
and bits of green algae clinging to our hair
when we dove in and swam its breath in the summer mornings!

Too big to carry, to unmanageable to grasp,
the wind roared past me and yelled,
"I'm staying, you couldn't even catch me if you tried.!"

Poet

Every part of me,
however weak or small,
is poet.

Every muscle fiber,
every vein,
is poet.

Every muscle yearns
because of it,
very drop of blood stings
from it,
is poet.

Every part of me,
my muscles and my blood,
my brain and soul,
every part of me that sighs
at sight of leaf, or grass, or sky.
every part of me that feels or sees
the wonders of life's miracles,
is poet.

1958

Post-processing

Poems are but snapshots
taken by the soul,
disparate images,
framed, shot, cropped,
developed over time,
patiently correcting
exposure, color temperature,
white balance, highlights, and shadows,
sharpening the image,
fiddling with the clarity
until one gets it right.

Free Verse

Thoughts came with their own form
and so, I wrote them down.
Although I was more comfortable
with song, with rhymes that fell
predictably in measures of their own.

And they became part of my litany,
a solace I could flee to, a season of my soul.
And once thus learned I took the words,
apportioned them to look like sonnets,
like the *coplas* of my youth.
But it was not the same, even in verse,
there's no such thing as free.

Locket

To be a poet, oh, I've fought it!
Judge and jury to my own fury!
Yet, it comes, and I can't stop it.
I open up the odious locket
and I see pictured my own truth.
But tell me, tell, where's the proof?

I Write

I was going through one of my transformations
barely cognizant of the emerging self.
I was cleaning out my closets,
Relining drawers, relining shelves,
Trying to recall all my previous selves.

It had been years since we'd been together.
Oh, we'd called, we'd written, kept in touch,
But a month ago we were face to face,
at last, together for two days.

She had remarried. she had a big house
and we had escaped to sit in her dressing room.

I still have the dress
I wore at your wedding, she said.
It's in the closet,
To the right of the window.

She began to open doors and drawers.
Fuchsia, red, turquoise, and black
Suddenly brightened the autumn light.

No, I said.
And did you know?
I write.

Introductions

I am a poet,
a mother,
a wife,
and erstwhile daughter.

I like
patterns,
in infinite,
finite form.

That's it.
That's me.

(Forgot to mention
that I like
Herbs de Provence
simmering
in a stew)

And you?

Family and Friendship

Family Ties

Molly Shelly's papa perished in the War
when she was only three.
He never saw her stroll her dolly
in the cart the made and painted red,
nor saw her brother, Jackson,
walk beside her
pretending they were wed.

"We are the parents now,"
they said walking in tandem,
down the lane.

Brother and sister,
they chose sister and brother
when the real time came,
staying close, sharing life,
he a sister's husband,
she a brother's wife.

Molly and Jackson Shelley married
William Henry and Mary Emma Askew
Molly and William Henry were my great grandparents

The War of the Rebellion, 1861–1865

My grandparents' grandfathers,
all, fought in that war.

And those who returned
to their farms and their families,
bewildered, discouraged, wounded,
made love to their wives
behind closed doors,
whispering "never forget"
and sobbing "always remember".

But they did, and they didn't.
So, their children
never understood
the meanest of their lives.

There were two Williams,
two Phillips, Two Benjamins.
A Joel, a Lewis James.

Three saddled their horses
and trotted into war.
Four marched or rode the rails,
One joined the Militia
and stayed his ground.

A minié ball caught
one William little distracted
just outside Atlanta, shattering one leg.
while in Kentucky, Yankees caught the other one
and sent him down to Vicksburg for exchange.

The two named Phillip
lasted out the War,
galloping, cantering, trotting their horses,
then finally walking them home.

Both Benjamins lay moribund
long days and nights, prisoners,
trembling from cold and memories.
One was sick of body,
and one was sick of mind,
but only one survived to tell the story.

Lewis James Johns had four slaves,
four children, a wife, and
a comfortable farm and life.
Yet in the summer of sixty-three
he left them all to join the Cavalry,
Tenth Regiment Georgia, Company E.

Joel Pinckney Yates,
Hickory Level Postmaster, Militia District Six,
Had ten children and one on the way
in April, eighteen sixty-one.
Too old to fight, he Joined the Militia and stayed.

The Battle of Croix Rouge Farm

July 26, 1918

When your feet quit growing,
I will knit you some socks
with the very needles
my own grandmother gave me,
so many years ago.

I can't see well anymore,
my grandmother had said
It's time for you to learn to knit.
We'll knit some socks.

She went to her closet and took out
an old biscuit tin. She opened it
and, ceremoniously, carefully,
I peered inside and saw
the set of fine small needles,
a half skein of yarn, and
an old, yellowed cutout of
newspaper print.

Red Cross Notice: All who have been
Knitting for the Red Cross are requested
to bring or send the knitted article in
by next week, as the chapter is anxious
to have them shipped.

Mrs. D. W. Boone
Chairman, Kitting

I had a brother who died in France,
you see, It was during the Great War,
you know. I was just a girl then,
no older than you are now, and
proud to do my part.
Don't know if he got them,
I'd like to think he did,
before he died, you know,
in the Battle of Croix Rouge Farm.

Pedigree

My father was a leprechaun,
my mother was the wind,
my birthplace was a far-off place
away from help of friend.

The muses, they abducted me
when I was four days old,
and made of me a prisoner
in castles made of gold.

And I grew up in loneliness
in my captivity,
and my melancholic world
knew not reality.

And now away from golden fields,
away from guardian Muse,
I'll sing my melancholic songs,
and put them all to use.

Empathy

When I was three I jabbed my sister's leg
With the rod of a feather duster. She was six.

I had grabbed it, I had jabbed my sister's leg
Accidentally, on purpose.
She howled, burst into tears.

I stared at her. A big welt on her leg,
a tiny spot of blood in the center.
I saw her pain.

I couldn't feel it, I gulped, burst into tears.
I'm sorry, I said, I didn't mean it.
I lied.
She looked at me then,
Said, "It's ok,"
and hugged me.

Trust

You are fearless, my daughter said,
Lowered her eyes, then looked away.
The children in the playground
Squealed and yelled across the street.
We stood watching them
from the second story window—

"Tengo miedo" I heard
echoing through the din of the playground.
"Tengo miedo," I heard whispered
through the walls of time,
through tears. I was five.

My sister, eight, stood,
ever further out of reach
by the edge of the slide.
I climbed each rung of those metal steps
clutching the one just beyond reach.

With each rung the antiphonal chorus echoed:
tengo miedo, a frightened whisper.
No tengas miedo, she yelled, "It'll be all right."

Headfirst I went, my pinafore
rumpled against the grain of the wood.
She ran—ran fast.
and as my hands reach out
to brace the fall,
she caught me.

The Gap

If I were seven then, he would have been thirty-four.
Perhaps I was eight, and he already thirty-five,
but maybe nine, as I remember it so well,
and he thirty-six.

The gap remained the same,
as did our hurried steps,
each of us running faster
down the hill.

The bus stood in wait for us,
the riders nervously watching
the little girl running
with her father, in tandem.

He laughed encouragingly
letting go of my hand
certain we were in step
every step of the way.

The Tell

I can tell we looked happy then,
both my mother and my big sister
smiling, one wistfully, one
expectant, my little brother
staring into space, my baby
sister doing the same,
and I with a look of taking it
all in - the camera, the photographer,
the bare walled room, and the
sillones stacked in the corner
for people to sit on when they
were photographed in the
provincial capital where we lived.

Long after rage almost
consumed me, long after
I could safely use my gas oven
without being tempted to pull a Plath,
long after I had accepted what
was unacceptable to everyone else,
I open the album and see

a Christmas photograph
for the folks back home.
A picture-perfect family,
to show and tell.

But you didn't tell us father, did you?
although you knew, you knew then,
I can tell by the self-satisfied half
smile in the still glossy photograph.

Life is a Winding Road

Break as you approach the curve
my father said, *and then*
take your foot off the gas as you enter it,
that's a girl, easy now.

My first time at the wheel
of his chartreuse Chevrolet.
It was mid-century America
in middle Georgia.

Desolate county roads. On either side
there were fields, farmhouses,
a couple of trees here and there
breaking the landscape.

We were going downhill
on the winding road and,
as an afterthought, he said,
That's only on the downhills.

On the way back, you'll see,
As you go uphill, just keep
your foot on the gas and,
pay attention.

Going to Grandma's Florida Home

Her kitchen always seemed to smell like onions in the fall,
with the slight vinegary aroma of chutney, she made
from the firm, green pears that grew in her garden.
It was a magical place

Winters at her house were cool and crisp,
dark green with live oaks branches reaching down
till they came to my waist as if to hug me.
Those oaks were where her peacocks roosted at night,
The ones she beckoned in a high falsetto,
Come, beautiful! Come, beautiful! She would say,
then they would slowly strut to her
with their feathers fanned out proudly.
It was a magical place

We'd drive into the yard in spring and stop short,
at the gate, not to miss the walk to her house,
running to and fro through fuchsia, orange,
salmon, pink, and white azaleas bushes
with flowers that tumbled down in the breeze,
fluttering about like a kaleidoscope.
It was a magical place.

Her front yard gave to the bay,
its brackish water so clear and quiet
we could see the oysters trying to hide
just a net away from our rowboat.
The fiddler crabs all golden, yellow, orange,
we sometimes managed to catch

once in a while in summer,
would wiggle past us, backing into
the little holes in the sand
that looked like pencil jabs.
It was a magical place.

Il Nonno Gazzano

The scent of jasmine mingles
with timbre of your voice
in the shadows of my memory.

Those mornings the sun caressed the air,
rising ever so slowly over
and above the pergola.

You sat, hands folded, looking
straight into my eyes,
listening, and then answering.

Your voice was raucous, flat,
heavy with the weight of years,
tinged with *Piemontese* rhythms.

We didn't converse—we chanted,
antiphonal responses to silent questions
which still echo in my heart.

In Celebration of my Argentine Childhood

Exquisite tenderness, passionate abandon,
persimmon-colored mornings dappled with light.

- So was my childhood, drenched in mauve longings,
jacarandas Octobers, and mulberry nights.

But that was another place,

Where clocks and watches shared the same name
and kept similar times, where
hope was the color of nascent
oranges and ripe, succulent limes.

Los relojes ran in tandem,
the big hand holding the little hand
joined at the center.
Time was not linear then
but circular, halved and quartered,
each sharing the same space.

And when hands came together
at mid-day *Mamá* made sure that
they were washed and clean
and as radiant as our face.

Carnavalito

The Andean music
flooded the flat landscape
of the schoolyard.
We stood at attention
and listened to the sad notes
that made their way
into our waiting hearts.

Our province was surrounded
by deep rivers not by gorges,
but we could imagine them,
the Indians who sat cross-legged,
playing their flutes into the distance.

And we felt one with them,
those flute players we imagined
with pitch black hair,
and broad, brown faces.

Our hair, blond or brown,
immigrant children, all of us,
was plaited, parted in the middle,
in imagined Indian fashion.

And when the music stopped
and then restarted,
we took our places, joined hands,
and broke into the sinuous
dance of the of Andean music.

Embarcadero

You did not ask; I did not tell you.
The river ran swiftly through our town,
and from the embarcadero,
I saw it upside down.

I can't say that it mattered,
I knew it would not last.
Its course would swell, engulf its borders,
its waters muddy, angry, rushing past.

El Rio Paraná

The river ran north-south, as most rivers do.
Its waters turbid, heavy with the weight
it had licked off the edges of
the upstream banks.

Soon, near evening,
the river would meander
through the islands
of its own creation,
fragmented, tired,
already tasting the salt
that would overtake
its sweetness.

Exile

I have been encased in ice, a flame
frozen in time and burning,
since crossing the river that night.

I have an image of a girl
leaning on the rail then turning to see
the lights of the city and the river's bend.

Her arms folded, leaning against the rail,
her head bent, hiding her tears,
tears that fell into the water,
the brown, brown water of the river,
leaving a silver trail.

A trail to be followed
so someday I could return
when all the ice was melted
by the flickering lights that burn
forever on the hillside
behind the river's bend,
a trail for me to follow
until my exile ends.

Family Historian

What was the name
of the man with overalls
who sat on a bench
in front of the store?
He always wore a hat.
He gave me candy.
Did he give you candy?

He sounds, across the cell towers,
a bit breathless, pondering,
and yet reluctant to call and ask.

"Yes, I remember the candy,"
his name was Don Humberto,
I say, pronouncing the name
in Spanish, and modulate my voice
to sound affirming.

The trick works.
His memory stirs, expands,
The colors coming into focus.

It was hard candy, wrapped,
He says,
And I always chose lemon.

Lost Children

We were lost children, hungry and cold.
We didn't hurt no one, we did as were told.
We never bought ice cream 'cause we couldn't pay
till they put it on sale, then it melted away.

It was always the two of us, and the raindrops falling,
I was always the two of us, and the future calling.

We had friends for dinner whenever we could.
The food was not fancy, but it sure was good,
with greens from a garden I tended myself
served on blue dishes from far away Delft.

The babies they came, so evenly spaced,
the pain each brought with him the others erased.
They came like the seasons, four in twelve years,
conceived in confusion, delivered in tears.

The future completed we turned to the past
in search of old dragons and slew them, at last.
The sins of our fathers will visit no more,
so, open the windows and unlock the doors.

Julie

Julie wants to climb a tree, she's only two years old.
She looks at me expectantly, afraid that I might scold.

Julie has a kitten that she picks up by the tail.
The kitten does not seem to mind, it hardly ever wails.

Julie wants to go outside in search of ladybugs,
but first she needs a little kiss and three tight little hugs.

Julie goes to Central Park with peanuts for the squirrels.
They all come out a-running, with jumps and little twirls.

Julie, Julie, not quite three, my precious namesake child,
so intrepid, so carefree, a challenge drives her wild.

He Loves a Dinosaur

I know a boy whom I adore.
My love is unrequited.
You see, he loves a dinosaur,
it's true; they're never parted.

Oh, all he does the whole day long
is to study books of lore
about that buried pile of bones,
the ancient dinosaur.

I long to call him up and say,
My love, you're so desirous!
But I refrain for he prefers
his favorite brontosaurus.

Both of Us Laughing

I used to be a schoolgirl, and then a woman,
and now I'm, oh, no!
I don't know what I am,
although I know I am your mother.
The echoing laughter
and the angle of your eyebrows
makes that undeniable.

All I know is that
I am no longer entrapped
in Ávila, between St. Theresa
and St. John,
unable to do anything about it
but write passionate letters,
and that for now
I am in Boston, with you,
high up in the safety of The Marriott,
room number 13-34,
not exactly a convent,
nor a Spanish medieval walled town,
and you say,

"Mummy, it's so good
to be with you like this,"
adult, no longer a kid,
and both of us laughing

A Mother's Silent Wish

To Hank - *on his 20ᵗʰ birthday*

I would like to tell you, tell you all you need to know
to see the sun rising through this blinding snow.

I would like to rock you, rock you till you fall asleep,
cover you with blankets warm, and soft, and deep.

I would like to cradle you (Oh yes!) in your mother's arms,
turn off all the strident noise, the blaring smoke alarms.

But instead, I'll say nothing, (Oh no!) nothing that you'll hear,
secretly gathering you to my breast, holding you near.

Find Your Own Way

Go where life leads you, find your own way!
I'll never leave you, I'm here to stay.

You won't find seagulls in the desert.
You won't find hawks way out at sea.
You won't find snowflakes in hot cinders,
won't find yourself inside of me.

My mirror shows just one reflection
revealing all I try to hide,
and life goes on in one direction,
with past future side by side.

And there they sit, like two big bookends.
Each one it looks the other way,
and in between are our life stories,
a brand-new page we write each day.

Don't read too much in what I'm saying,
don't seek your truth upon my face.
There's only one thing I can tell you,
only the present can erase.

All Thing Real Were Once Only Imagined

Daughter, let me not lose you! Is what I think sitting
on the porch of the Concord Inn drinking pink lemonade.

A transparent yellow half-moon of lemon deftly
ensconced on the rim. There are two colonial flags

hanging from the entrance. History and tradition,
quiet permanence frames my view.

Luisa May Alcott's house is just down the road.
Can it be? I was twelve when I first saw it in fiction,

Described in Spanish, by the light of my bed side lamp.
and you, when did I first imagine you?

And now, you're married, living in Concord
as did those Little Women a century ago.

Oh, let me not lose you! Is what I think, sitting
on the porch of the Concord Inn drinking pink lemonade.

I sip through the straw and watch the liquid
travel up, and the glass once again become transparent.

It's clear. I need your permission to keep you.

FaceTime

A lazy Sunday morning with Anna
reading picture books on FaceTime.
You can read, she said, *I can turn the pages.*
We held our devises tight.

Two thousand miles away,
five states between us, her sister and
brother each in their rooms reading
chapter books, a thousand of miles away.
But she is still little, still wants to snuggle
with her mother close beside her
reading pictures books with Nanna,
two thousand miles away.

A Priori Statement

Three husbands, nine lovers, five children,
friends that pull in all directions
- Add rivalries only siblings know.

And yet, *our love is an unspoken constant!*
is what you said in response to a letter I wrote.

I tromp around the wilderness
my state struggles to protect,
and what I see is the cutoff
we used to take to school.

I hear the melody of those far-off mornings,
I feel the vaporous unguent
rise from the humus of the forest and
bathe my soul with memory.

My step quickens as I walk,
my heartbeat becomes audible,
I glance down and think I
see you at my side.

Our love is an unspoken constant!
is what you said, and
as I hike along the wilderness,
it's in the stillness of the forest that
I best remember, the silent
a priori statement
indelibly inscribed in our distant hearts.

Cymbals

We will grow old together,
tucking our childhood
safely away.

The scent of camphor, surreptitiously escaping
from the armoires where we've secretly
stored our longings, seems to be calling us,
becoming auditory, mingling smell with sound,
confusing the senses.

We call, we write, we plan,
we set dates, we meet.
Sisters, sheltering, seeking shelter.

Dreams collide with accomplishments,
cymbals ringing, the two of them,
the two of us, concave circles
so long sheltering our kin, our youth,
bursts with sound resounding.

Wanderings

Troubadour

I don't want for money, I don't want for time,
I just want to sing my tunes using simple rhyme.

I drift and I drift, I never stay long.
I work my piece; I sing my song.

What if someday you're proven wrong,
drift toward a place where you belong?

If there's a place such as you say
then for my lodging I will pay.

You know the currency, the price?
Oh, yes, hot fire! Oh, yes, cold ice.

Directions

Where are you?
At the edge of Rhetoric. Next to Tomorrow.
What road do I take to reach you?
Take Yesterday.

And if I lose my way?
Follow the swallows.
They always remember the way to my door.

So, if you lose your way,
you must wait until spring,
and come to me flying
on a swallow's wing.

A Good Place to Live Is a Good Place to Die

For the past three mornings I have awakened twenty-five stories high in the
middle of a city looking down over church steeples, treetops, and roof gardens.

Boston was squat, red bricked, with carefully delineated streets, framed by the Charles
with little sails boats bobbing by.
And now, I'm in Montreal, the city below me a jumble
of concrete, copper roofs - matte green, and the thicket of the royal mountain straight ahead.

I think in every city there are those who have never crossed its gate, and I'm reminded once again of the old man in Paris who smiled to me with pride and said:

Je ne suis jamais sorti de mon quartier à moi. El moi, j'y resterai là jusqu'à ma morte.

I looked at him in amazement when I realized he was serious and had never left his neighborhood.

He could read my face, for he said, in French, of course,

It's truly normal, that. A good place to live is a good place to die.

Chalone Vineyards, 1980

Feel just like a feather floating in the breeze.
The day is full of sunshine, and I'll do as I please.

Wine, wine, Burgundy, Bordeaux,
Wine, wine, Zinfandel, Pinot.

Don't have no connections that might tie me down,
I'll pack up my things and I'll go out of town.

Sparrow Hawk Mountain is half a day away.
Think I'll visit Kevin and taste his Chardonnay.

Such utter desolation, such mystical retreat,
with solitude so near communion seems complete.

California vineyards all cry - Come taste my wine!
While hidden by the Pinnacles, the best waits on the vine.

Cottondale

Cottondale, twenty-two miles from Youngstown,
where U.S. Highway two-thirty-one
runs flat, East-West, with the Bay Line tracks

parallel, to the right.
Oh, Sao Paulo seems so far away,
its hills so steep to climb!

This stretch of road will lead me there,
will lead me to Sao Paulo
here the hills await.

But first a ship must sail,
a ship which waits for me
at the end of the Bay Line rail.

Just as you've waited, waited for me,
somewhere between Sao Paulo,
between Sao Paulo and Cottondale.

Oleander Scented Memories

Bitter leaf, sweet blossom,
sea gulls flying out to sea.
Jekyll Island in the fifties,
wanting bourbon, drinking tea.

I became your sweet possession,
and you paid the bitter fee.
Jekyll Island in the fifties
was what I was meant to be.

Cross Iowa Bicycle Run, 1997

Bicycles back lit in Iowa City,
photographed squinting
into the sun.
The row askew
and temporary
after an early morning run.

Outside invisible gates
to the city
is where the endless prairie lies
unsuspecting it's judge
and jury
to whatever the soul tries.

Floridian Woods

Silence interrupted by a hoot owl's call,
the air so thick you can watch feathers fall.

Sunlight filtering through palm trees and pine
reflecting shadows long and wide.

Fragrant, musty walkways that take shape as I go,
these are the Florida woods I know!

Frogs and turtles plopping in and out of water,
stillness suspended by a redbird's flutter.

Shimmering, slithering snakes, lazy and slow.
These are the Florida woods I know!

At the Station

There you stood, waiting for me.
The crowd pushed and shoved
and hurried through the busy station.

Outside a soft rain was falling,
nearly invisible, moist.

Memories of conversations crowded out all else.
Snatches and snippets
of shared laughter, of tears, of stories,
tugged, pushed, and shoved racing away in front of me.

I ran. I ran straight into your arms
and held you close.

So, you're here, you said.
I knew you'd come.

Atlanta

I am awash with memories of you,
memories suffused with dreams,
dreams now become memories.

Today, I walk through your neighborhoods,
your Peachtrees, your malls,
and I recall growing up Georgian in the sixties.

Baseball uniforms and baseball bats,
Martin, and we shall overcome,
world-class ambitions, homespun.

Transformation, pride,
red clay and green kudzu
meeting concrete and glass.

Marthasville,
Terminus,
Atlanta!
All grown up now,
Sparkling,
Foxy lady with class.

Gentle and Proud

Gentle and proud,
your little-girl gait
is measured and calm.

The wind from the highlands
whistles as you walk,
whistles right past you and you turn to look.

Where are going, Wind, leaving me behind?
to the plains and the lowlands,
where the yellow flowers hide.

Sleepless Chilean Nights

Sleepless nights
and you cry out to me.

I'm wide awake
and through the silence
I hear you scream.
Huahua! My huahuita!
Yet, Garcilaso tells us
only mothers used that word
in Inca times.
Huahua! My huahuita!

Sleepless night
and I reach out to you.

I take your hand
and with it make a fist
against your palm.

Huahua! My huahuita!

Barcelona

I love this city, this natural port,
with oil-slicked waters, and cranes to abort

cargo and garbage from foreign made ships
full of tired sailors with lies on their lips.

What's there to life but to be, but to feel,
fleeing contrivance for something that's real.

The Core of the Sunset

I had forgotten about sunsets out at sea,
days away from shore,
when light diffracts into
yellow, green, persimmon, turquoise, red,
as the sun reveals its core.

Mejillones

The taste of saffron and *pimentón*
was unexpected.
Torremolinos at twilight,
the town pausing
to catch its breath
before beginning again.

The beach deserted,
our daughter
fast asleep,
exhausted from
a day of play.

And we, novices,
eager to try,
yet reluctant,
tasted the broth,
the mussels,
and mouthed the foreign,
newly learned word,
Mejillones

Mijas

Mijas, its whitewashed houses
crowded in the hills
look like a band of doves
nestled in a tree above the sea,

The streets ahead so steep
the window boxes below
are level with my hand
should I reach out.

Our children ride on donkeys
through narrow streets.
I follow behind and say,
Arre, arre, burro
stay in line.
the donkeys stop.

We walk together
down the hill,
you now alongside of us,
augmented caravan.

The promontory waits.
The hills plunge down,
the dry, parched plain
rushes thirstily
to sea.

In the distance
the Mediterranean meets the sky,
their blues, blending
becoming indistinct.

I feel your shoulder next to mine.
and then, a slight embrace
as memory
converts to consciousness.

Arre, arre, memory...
Stay in line.

Drizzle

Cole Porter knew that in summer, Paris sizzles,
and in winter Paris drizzles.
The French call it *la bruine.*
But if the drizzle is hardly a drizzle,
and you know it will last all day,
you leave your *parapluie* at home
and simply weather *le crachin.*

In the North Carolina Mountains
there are warm drizzles, cold drizzles,
here one minute and gone the next drizzles,
all day drizzles, icy drizzles,
steamy drizzles, sudden drizzles, and,
you can feel them coming drizzles.
Drizzles—all sorts—and I wonder if
had Franz Boaz studied the Cherokees
instead of the Inuit, would he have found
there were as many words
for drizzle as the Inuit had for snow.

Memory of a Viennese Morning

Life is circuitous. Like conversations,
images converging in juxtaposition,
dangling participles, mixed metaphors,
inside jokes, and ethnic slurs,
leaving the listener wondering.

As we rounded the corner,
Our arms full of Christmas presents,
the wind blowing cold and crisp against my face,
I turned to watch the traffic light
And caught her eye.

Days like today, she said,
remind me of you, the sunshine
pale yellow against your face
reflecting the snow of a Viennese morning.

Restoring My Circadian Rhythm

Jet lag in full swing, chills, and nausea,
cortisol levels adjusting to new diurnal variations,
I pause a second or two and let my eyes adjust
to the light of an autumnal Paris sky.
I have returned. Like a local in *la rentrée*
into the crowd and up the metro steps of St Michel
as though I belong.

I stumble into Gibert Jeune to buy the latest *Prix Goncourt*,
then out the door, turn right and pass
the inexpensive hotel du Mont Blanc
where I had stayed once in my student days.
I glance at the marquee of Théâtre de la Huchette
Ionesco, perhaps, I think, *perhaps this trip*,
and then turn left, past the Greek gyros,
the Moroccan couscous places.
Every building on that street a restaurant of sorts.

And left again. *St. Severin*
a bicycle propped casually against its iron fence,
while to one side, a man is playing a guitar,
his open guitar case hinting for euros.
The church stands as solitary as the hermit
in whose honor it was built, as quiet as if
it had taken a vow of silence. Its *cloche* is silent too.

I enter, the wooden chairs crowed
into two neat rows leading me to the altar,
the stain glass windows letting in a muted light.
My eyes adjust to the penumbra and
I think of all the pilgrims who have made their way

To St Severin to start their journey.
And how, how am I that different?

I kneel in reverence, then stand and turn to leave.
I glance up at the old round clock that quietly sits
under the sixteenth century organ.
The minute hand moves gently down toward center.
Two thirty. I'm wide awake.

Blue Vinyl

A weekend in Paris, and then, there was rain.
Ah, Paris, ah, Paris, to be there again!

The change did me good. It was just what I needed.
for too long it'd been just sameness, repeated.

We walked to the Galleries and there bought a hat.
We couldn't afford much more than that.

The hat was blue vinyl with big, floppy rim.
It was just sheer indulgence, bought on a whim.

A weekend in Paris, a hat for the rain,
and each time I wear it, its Paris, again.

Deauville

Somewhere
between Deauville and morning
sometime
Between youth and goodbye
someone
I will always remember
answered me
but never asked me why.

La flâneuse réticente

The summer I spent in that small French town,
I seldom wandered far from *mon quartier a moi,*
But one day I turned left instead of right,
and then kept going, unafraid, a slight frisson
of adventure, apprehension, quickening my steps.

I came upon a street that was lined with shops -
A jumble of genres - a bakery, a toyshop next door,
shoe repair, dress shop, meat market selling sausages,
a jewelry store, flowers for sale in one that sold seeds.

I wandered in and out of shops,
then doubled back, returning.
The street gave to a square where
men sat smoking, leisurely, eyes closed,
hats pulled down against their noses
shaded by large plane trees, decades old.

Saint Tropez

The sun at St. Tropez shines
with a garish light
upon the faded buildings
on the shore.

And two blocks down,
at Place the Lices,
we watch the locals
play their game of boules
as a crowd gathers around
to cheer them on.

We sip Pernod,
then eat our *moules*
and there await the night.
For you and me
somehow
this moment had to come
for things to be all right.

Poppies

I'll gather the poppies that grow in the spring
I'll weave them together to make you a ring,
I'll take my guitar and a song I will sing
of all the joys our tomorrows will bring.

For tomorrow will be full of laughter,
yes, tomorrow will be full of song,
for I know that forever after
in your arms is where I belong.

I've wandered so far from the land of my birth!
I've sold my possessions for half of their worth
and traveled the world, its length, and its girth
seeking the difference 'tween sorrow and mirth.

I once passed the stile of a house in North France
exactly like one I'd seen, quite by chance,
while guiding a troupe of folkloric dance
through Montevideo with Monsignor Lance.

I saw a Greek laughing. I'd seen that before.
It's always the same, whether inland or shore.
Don't mean to belabor the point, or to bore,
but each man was standing front of his store.

That stile and that laughter, they each kept me out.
They filled me with questions, they filled me with doubt.
Stay away, don't come closer, they both seemed to shout.
That fence was protection, that laughter was clout.
But sorrow's been different each time that we've met.
Its masks and disguises I just can't forget
cause they've both been dropped with little regret,
in place of signs saying *we've got rooms to let.*

The Many Others
in Our Lives

At the Seaside

Sea oats swaying on the sand dunes,
seaweed tickling my toes,
sea gulls flying high above me,
sea waves swiftly o'er me roll.

Children making sandy castles,
lovers kissing in the sun,
old men fishing from the harbor.
All of this, and I see all.

Caught Unaware

From the Andalusian promontory
we could see Africa, beyond the sea,
suffused with light and mist.

The hills behind us, still lush and green,
went unnoticed for I was imagining
Morocco, the Sahara, the Nile.

Until the hunters appeared.

Buenos días, señora, they said,
touching the tips of their hats
and looking away, toward the hills,

Toward the birds that were resting
before their flight
which would take some of them
to the warmth and solace
of perpetual light.

Nikon N 90

Woman of a certain age
is standing waiting at a bus stop,
corner of King Street and Queen
Charleston, S. C.

She turns her head and sees a woman,
not much younger, coming straight at her.
And that woman is me.

She wanted to be shot and revealed
admired for her smile
or the hat she wore jauntily
tilted slightly to one side

I could tell

I point at her,
about to shoot her,
Nikon, N90, no flash.
Should I move for you lady?
she says with a wink,
Or maybe,
are you shooting me?

Cheap Women

Cheap women don't age well,
those who steal husbands in their youth,
they tend to find fulfillment shopping
instead of in the arts, now, how uncouth!

You hardly recognize them, later on,
their jowls beginning to appear,
dressed up expensively from head to toe,
their too tight clothes riding up their rears.

Coping With Change

The doe returned to the clearing,
the same nonchalant swagger,
insouciant as yesterday.
I dropped my trowel
and stood to face her.

She turned her head,
lowered her gaze,
shook her head,
and made her way past me
toward the birches.

She began to nibble,
delicately, methodically,
swaying the branches.
her eyes meeting mine,
in defiance, seemed to say:

Those branches you trimmed yesterday
and tossed carelessly away to wither
were my favorites. No matter.
I am resilient. these branches are higher,
*harder to reach. But they are **mine.***

Florida Transplant

I was one of *them Florida folks come to the mountains,*
not one of them, but I'd do. And how was I to know
that when you admired a plant it was dug up,
put in a bucket for you to take home and treasure?

I was slow to learn, but I did, that once flowers had faded,
they were allowed to seed, the seeds allowed to ripen,
carefully inspected and watched, and when good and dry, snipped.

I knew I could expect seeds come late June
when my neighbor, said, *Yes, them there foxgloves*
I've had since Mama saved me some seeds first year we married,
and I'll tell you what when they come in, I'll gather you some,
then we'll wait for the right moon to plant them.

By end of summer the tiny, velvety plants,
had begun to break ground, waiting for spring,
when they would vie with each other for space,
and spend the summer growing, each at its own pace.
And I? What did I know of plants? Of mountain ways?
That come every October you proceeded to dig up seedling
setting them out for the next season?

Soon my garden was resplendent with
Ruth's biennial foxgloves, sweet Williams
from the seeds Kenneth had gathered,
day lilies Marvin had thinned out from his garden,
wild raspberries Joe had dug up on Otter Road.

Ruth died several years back.
I moved just a mountain away last fall
taking with me seeds, cuttings, seedlings,
and memories.
And now its October again, time to round up
and transplant foxgloves and sweet Williams,
thin out the day lilies, throw out some seeds.

Focal Point

He leaned into me,
his wide welt corduroy jacket,
the color grass after the first frost,
almost brushing against my cheek.

Look left, look right, look up, look down,
the ophthalmologist said.
I couldn't help it.
I noticed his slacks, his socks.

They were the same, mute green
that matched his jacket exactly.
His shirt was starched, crisp white,
but his neatly tied bow tie
was a geometric design
in every color of the rainbow.

The Potpourri

The potpourri in the living room
is full of myriad petals of roses spent.

I open the lid and smell
the scent they didn't have
when they sat in glass vases
reflecting the sunshine
of the open window.

They were beautiful once,
in their freshness,
but now, somehow,
pungent with memories
are dearer to me still.

Each petal the vestige
of apologies for words unkind,
love expressed only
through bouquets-by-wire,
or the celebratory expectancy
of guests.

The Florida Soft Shell Turtle

(Apalone ferox)

She swims awkwardly
gaining the shore of the stream
that flows from the big, deep lake
all the way to the sea.

She won't go that far. She
only needs to get to shore.
a foothold first, then she
swings up the other paddle-feet.

The grassy slope smooths out.
A sandy patch is just ahead.
Her front feet down for purchase,
her back feet dig.

A crow sits on a cypress branch
and watches her, quiet at first,
then caws to his brothers.

The sand and grass fly through the air,
the greenish dust enclosing her.
Impervious, she continues. Almost through,
the nest now deep enough,

she sits, her snout high as if to savor
spring's mid-day clear, crisp air.
She is done. And now to cover them
a bit, with sand, with errant strands of grass.

She leaves, then turns,
one last look, neck outstretched,
hurrying back to the safety of the lake.

She does not see the crows
landing one by one, greedy beaks
poised to feast.

Mary Louise

Tall and slender was Mary Louise
with long and stringy hair.
her yellowish teeth showed when she sneezed
and she walked with a lofty air.

She had nine children, this Mary Louise,
and a husband to beat her, she had.
her eyes they were crossed, her legs knock-kneed,
yet, she'd say, *Life isn't so bad.*

Sunday Brunch

It's a gorgeous summer morning.
I am enjoying eggs Benedict
discounting every guilty calorie as if
I didn't care, looking straight ahead and
over the shoulder of my companion
who is toying with his huevos rancheros.

I see him stop to read the menu
posted at the sidewalk café while
surreptitiously glancing at the diners
as he walks slowly by,

He's a big, big man,
an erect beached whale,
black shirt, neatly pressed,
a brown leather belt,
looped into tan trousers,
brown leather shoes, freshly shined,

His wife, close to his side, trim,
narrow of waist, wide of hips,
resembles a mermaid idly
swimming by, encircling him.
They are strolling
on a leisurely Sunday morning,
trying to decide.

The Egret

The egret stands, a question mark,
and peers into the creek.
The fish swim by unnoticing
the predatory beak.

The beak goes down, and up it comes,
the fish is in midair!
Too big a fish to swallow whole,
it missed by just a hair.

The egret stands, a question mark,
and shakes his greedy beak,
then picks the fish back up again,
and throws him in the creek!

The Therapist

Don't ask me to tell you any-
thing. All I know is erased
by that little dance of
yours as you reach for
a clean piece of paper
to jot something down.

Light in your room is al-
ways diffused and filtered
through layers and layers
of hours the contents of
which I know nothing about.

Why do I tell you any-
thing?
But I do, and watch
you change the angle of
your eyes as if to see
only the last utterance
throwing everything else
out of focus.

You think that
we are talking, you and I, but
no. That's not it. What
we are doing is constantly
changing F stops,
bracketing images that our
words just imagined.

The Women Are the Working Bees

Sparrow Hall–Winslow Homer 1881–1882
National Gallery of Art, Washington, D.C.

Winslow Homer, landscape painter,
printmaker, watercolorist, lithographer,
Harper's battle scene and campfire
sketch artist throughout the Civil War,
takes a break from documenting
a torn country trying to repair itself
and sets off to England with his watercolors
settling in the small village of Cullercoats.

He doesn't hide here, but explores,
rendering what he sees in watercolors.
One morning, on his wandering, he stops short.
As he rounds the corner of Sparrow Hall
he quietly takes out his pad and pencil.
He is once again impressed by the women
of the town who are so busy that
they ignore him as he stands there sketching.
His pencil flies on the page. He makes
mental notes of the pinks, the grays,
the muted greens and blues, the plaids.

There is a woman sitting by a door where
bottles hang, as if in display. Is it a tavern?
Her sleeves rolled up. She is quietly writing,
or seems to be to our modern eyes.
Further down, six steps up there is an open door.
On either side there are young women knitting.
one on the left, on the stoop, and one the right,
standing a bit lower, on a barrel. A redheaded

woman comes to the door and says something
to the girl on the barrel, who listens and responds.
Down the steps a little girl is holding on
to a toddler, the younger child teasing
a cat with a piece of yarn. The cat
is asleep, and one can almost hear him snore.

The artist slips away, unnoticed, and on his way
back home decides that watercolor just won't do.
He thinks of his easel, his oils, and the colors
he will use, the light as he remembers it.
His thoughts wander back to the women
Of Sparrow Hall, now etched in his mind.
None of the women saw him. He is certain.
Each of them busy with their own lives.

The Tiercelet

I am sitting in my back porch
shaded by two huge live oaks,
having a nightcap and feeling smug,
a bit superior I'll admit that too.

I've just remembered a word in French
I learned by chance reading Maupassant,
and marvel at how clever the French
can be with their descriptive nouns.

In English that would be rendered thirdling, I think,
and watch the two barred owls, side by side,
both the same size, clutching a thick oak limb,
one all fuzz and wobble, one sleek feathered, calm.

The owlet waits for a call, and when it comes, it's not
the familiar *Who-cooks-for you,* but something else,
an auditory nudge that pushed him forward. Then he lets go
knowing his father will fly down and catch him should he fall.

The mother, on the other tree, three times bigger
than the *tiercelet* watches attentively his approach.
He lands, he wobbles, shakes his heads, fluffs his feathers.
Both parents proud he's landed safely, and so am I.

To a Primer

I shall turn your brittle pages,
on this rainy, rainy day,
those old pages, dry as sedges,
dry as sedges, dry as hay.

Ah, your scent overflows my being,
it is crisp, like salty air,
as I sit alone and dreaming
of when I was young and fair.

Once you too were young, remember?
I was only six years old
on that day in mid-September
when your story you first told.

But now I am old and withered,
withered as a dried-up brook,
just an old man, gray and withered,
sighing over you, my book.

Maybe Tomorrow

The red shouldered hawk
has been coming to the garden.
He doesn't alight with grace.
He tumbles head and shoulders first
into the tender narrow leaves
of the spiderwort plant.

The lizards know to scamper
as he tries to re-position
but he pecks away anyway
hoping to find
some elusive prey.

Oh, what frustration,
what fury he exhibits!
A veritable toddler
trying desperately to reach
the cookie on the counter.

And just like a child
who has not gotten his way,
he shakes a bit,
raises his wings,
fans his tail
and flies off to a nearby post
to sulk and ponder.

The Serendipity Of Joy

Christmas Angel

Joy returns, imperceptibly,
contraband stowed away in grocery sacks
my children empty by the fragrant stove.

Once again, the scent of cinnamon, nutmeg,
cardamom, and mace perfume the air.
The Christmas tree,
so high it meets the ceiling, twinkles brightly.

We hum carols absentmindedly
as we decorate the cookies
with colored frosting, with sprinkles.

Then I hear her say, *Remember!*
Red is for Rudolph's nose,
And I get to decorate the angels.
I'm the oldest.

June's First Storm

Joy returns, *Feux d'artifice gratuit*,
count the miles, but slowly,
one, two, three, then add one thousand
before the digit to lend it cadence.

Wait for the thunder.

The oak trees crack into pieces
impaling the soggy turf, listen!
Soon the yard will be strewed
with chartreuse branches that glisten
with the weight of wetness
of Orlando summers.

Listen to those rain drops, listen!
Heavy, real, rolling playfully, joyfully
into the sand discreetly covered
with St. Augustine grass
which has been fertilized quarterly,
trimmed weekly, and neatly,
by the yuppy crew of yardmen
wearing matching polos with
clever little logos up their sleeves.

July Walk at Nightfall

Joy returns, leading its own parade,
absentmindedly skipping along
the swirly sidewalks of Rio.

But tonight, is not a Brazilian night
although the same mauve, yellow,
aquamarine light shines
under the halo of a nearly full moon.

It's just that January's river
runs deep within me,
flooding me with memories,
pushing me toward gladness.

It was in Rio that the sidewalks
all lead to open doors,
and songs, song there were sweeter
than ever before.

But tonight, is not a Brazilian night
although the same swirly sidewalks
stretch out before me
under the halo of a nearly full moon.

I feel the rhythm of my life resume,
and the lilting cadence of my days,
Jubilant, proud, with Portuguese accented
happiness resound.

Lady's Man

Joy, that's what you are.

We walk along the beach,
your Delft Blue eyes
squinting in the sun.

I, a man's woman,
You, a lady's man.

Mujeriego, I say,
Mujeriego,
eso es lo que eres.
Yes, a lady's man
is what you are.

Over and under
and up and down
you, and I, the sea,
we coalesce.

The waves encroach
Upon the sand
and all the riddles
that I've pondered on
suddenly make sense.

¿Comprendes?
Now I understand.

Last Run of the Day

The village below is an architect's maquette
of tiny houses, tiny avenues, tiny steeples,
tangled in errant ribbons of light.
The iridescent sunset weaves into
the fabric of the town.

That's where you are.
That's where I'll be.

I make my last descent
as I traverse, silently,
the undulating landscape,
slipping in and out
of shadows cast by
the crisscrossing slopes.

Joy slips in,
gliding beside me
as night and snow
begin to fall,
simultaneously,
azure and white.

The Pileated Woodpeckers
in the Old Dead Tree

She peeks out of the oblong hole
high up the old dead tree,
Chirp, chirp, chirp, she falters.

Her brother joins her, first
tentative and silent, then
his beak opens
and out it comes,
fractions of seconds behind,
and slightly deeper.

There are two voices now,
a chirp and an—ah tah, tah, tah!
Louder, and almost
in unison, but not quite.

I stand below, quiet and
squinting, looking at the nest,
trying to register
the nuances of their cries.

And counterpoint to the
insistent chirping,
Joy returns—quiet and deep
Settling in, in unison,
but not quite, with wonder.

The Brown Water Snake

Nerodia taxispiota

A slithering tangle of snakes
sunning by the side of the stream.

And oh, the joy
that breaks the quietness!

For they have returned,
to lie again in beds
of their own choosing,
of ochre-brown cypress,
hiding in plain sight
as hawks circle above
in confusion.

The Gardens of Earthly Delights

I'm standing at the Prado
studying a Bosch,
my eight-year-old transfixed,
he stands on tiptoes,
a little closer.

The tepid breeze
through the open window
tousles his stubborn hair.
He shakes his head and says,
Here-on-ee-muss
in pensive cadence.

His small and wiry arm
reaches out pointing first
to one panel, then the next.
He steps back, already knowing
just what to do to gain perspective.
Mom, he says, looking up at me,
Mom,

Joy -deep, and overriding centuries,
awe at the breath of life,
mingle with the slight breeze
coming from the window,
as he brushes his hair away
and turns to say,
I like Bosch.

Existential Ponderings

At the Gate

I feel better now. For so long
choice and possibility waited at the gate,
sometimes calling, sometimes knocking,
oh, I heard, but said, please wait.

I have built myself a mansion
with huge lawn I keep with care.
while I'm pruning, while I'm weeding,
I pretend that you aren't there.

I'm too discouraged. I'm too confused,
too overwhelmed with worry.
I keep ad-libbing, keep improvising
to stay true to my story.

An understudy for too long,
afraid to play my part,
I keep ad-libbing, keep improvising
the lines I've learned by heart.

But I'm through with pretending,
with playing the lyre,
with hiding in smoke screens
of my heart's own fire.

I know that you're waiting,
there, at the gate.
Oh, call me, oh, call me!
I won't hesitate.

Adolescence

The moon is nearly full
and there's a start beside it,
twinkling bright.
I feel that I could throw
a pebble at the moon,
and it would reach, tonight.

May, 1959

Arriving At Last to My Mountain Retreat

I am in a cold, dark mood, wishing I could tell you
a little secret that I filed away in my hidden place,
that place marked *future use.*

The rain falls intermittently splattering
the windshield with liquid dust.
I flip the wipers on.
That only creates concentric circle halves,
residue thrown out by lorry tires
that snake around the hills and mountains
that are my home.

What I want to tell you is as invisible
as the other half of the sludgy windshield circle
I'm looking through.

The road I've traveled started
in the plains and has climbed
up the page on the map without a turn.
Straight up through cities
and tacky communities of neon and light.
Tout droit, Tout droit,
I've stayed on course.

But the road markers keep changing.
I glance toward them as they appear.
Where am I? I-75, F-73, C-5, S-575
and then, abruptly, one signpost disappears
In place of another.

Au même temps

It takes a lifetime to reflect
on one's missteps—
to discover too late
the secrets others kept.

They, the cognoscenti,
I, the inconnue,
ever the stranger,
even to myself.

Languages I would come to know
entrapped me even then,
when it all began,
to the place where I return, quotidian.

Nouns bordered by adjectives,
sometimes before, sometimes after,
never knowing, deep, deep down
their place.

And I, trapped between them,
trying desperately to see them both,
Au même temps.

After a Good Rain

After a good rain
I will weed my garden.
The earth is somnolent
and yielding then.

After a good cry
I'll ponder on forgiveness,
dry my tears
as I count to ten.

Change

The streets weren't paved then,
And men wore guns in holsters,
Downtown - right here.
she said and pointed to the church.

And that was fifty years ago.
Why, I remember when a man
Was shot right here.
It was during a fight
(And he was white!), and then,
They hanged the man who did it.
Just lynched him that same day.
And that was fifty years ago.

The parsonage is gone. It's been torn down,
but on that day, it was newly painted white.
Mother and I sat on the front porch swing
and watched the ladies in Sunday best pass by
and listened to the parson's wife talk about her town.
And then, we smoothed our gloves, and held our hats in place
as we got up and walked up to the church, next door.

Emphases change.
what once seemed so important
seems quite innocuous now.

I still remember
the word *ethnic* being esoteric,
and now it has become so common place.
The word *syndrome* used to be too clinical
to use in common speech.
And now, in reading <u>Time</u> I see

the word *avuncular* is used
describing presidential candidates.

I shiver with foreboding.
It's no good
if uncles run the show.

Disillusion

I kept thinking one day I'd wake up
and the feeling would be gone.

Instead, the sea gulls circled and swept
outside my window, never giving
a moment's peace. The sun rose to my left
and the waves slapped against the wall,
sloshing the windows with brackish might.

The crowded markets that lined the avenues
came to mind, where shopkeepers
hawking their wares in rising counterpoint,
had not persuaded me to buy.

Capernaum

Soon it will be summer
and the rains will start,
and the rains will find me
with an empty heart.

Gone will be the sorrow,
gone will be the pain
sitting there, like boulders,
damming up the rain.

Rain –the fields will flower.
Rain –the flowers bloom.
Rain will bring the hour
we'll reach Capernaum.

Fragile Spirit

I have a fragile spirit. I need a gentle song.
I'm oh, so weak and troubled, I need someone who's strong.

So come and walk beside me, I'll listen while you sing.
Oh, honey's sweet. It's tempting, but honeybees, they sting.

I'm penitent and weeping, confession trips my tongue,
I'm vulnerable and seeking to sing a different song.

So come and walk beside me, please listen while I sing.
Oh, honey's sweet. It's tempting. but honeybees, they sting.

Floridian Spring

That was another time, when April lasted all year,
and snakes were unafraid
to wander in and out of open doors
as they slithered in the yard,
preoccupied, it seemed,
on just where they should lay their eggs.

Sweet jacaranda blossoms stained the path
which came to our door,
the path the children used to tricycle to and fro,
as I sat on the steps, watching,
and let the fragrance of magnolia and confederate jasmine
strip away my winter and clothe my nakedness.

Gingerbread Girl

Half-baked excuses for running away,
feeling a bit burned, afraid of being spurned,
although I am sweet, although I am nice.
Sugar and spice.

I run and I run, and never get caught.
I am oh so careful and do what I ought.

I ran away from the Georgians shouting *Nigger!*
I ran away from the guy who pulled the trigger.
I ran away from my sister who was bigger.
I ran away from the boyfriend who was meaner.

I can run away from you, I think.
If I have just enough, enough to drink.

I can run away, I can I can
Taste me carefully.
See how fast I ran.

Iridescent

I am an amalgam
forged with pain.
I've tried to deny it
again, and again.

I am a rainbow
stretched out end to end,
thin layers of color
that know how to bend.

Leisurely

Let me drink life to its fullest
sipping leisurely each drop.
Let me pause and taste its flavor,
let this senseless gulping stop!

Oh, to drink for pleasure only,
not to quench a senseless thirst,
but because the cup is tempting,
not because somehow, I must.

Past Perfect

She said *I'm a survivor*
She didn't say I have survived.
She said *I'm a survivor.*

She was quiet for a minute
and didn't say more. I pictured her,
drifting out at high seas,
not safe, looking back to the shore.

She must have seen my puzzled look
Because she said, *well, you are too!*
Just think of all that you've been though.
You lived through those discrepancies ...

She said, you too are a survivor.
She didn't, say you have survived.
She said, you too are a survivor.

I calmly said, *no, I am not a noun,*
But an active verb, past perfect.

Pas de Deux

There is no sadness in my soul,
only the mist of the morning rising,
a pas de deux, an empty stage,
fluttering sounds of a heron flying.

There is no waiting at the door
listening for steps that might be falling,
or keeping coffee on the stove
in hopes that someone might be calling.

There is just peace, a joyful heart,
that's full and overflowing,
that rises early, meets the dawn,
and breezes gently blowing.

Tapestry

When illusion and reality entwine
and this tapestry I'm weaving becomes mine,
will I recognize it then by its design?

Ah, me, I've tangled so the yarn I must employ
unraveling threads of sorrow to find joy.

The Thorn of a Rose

Some of us lead double lives, some of us triple.
Some of us never make waves, not even a ripple.

Content to imagine, and dream, I suppose.
Afraid to be pricked by the thorn of a rose.

Invitation to Tea

I live in a house of wonder
with huge prairies hid within,
where the sunshine and the windstorms
fence with swords, strong, long, and thin.

I live where the cold can't harm me,
I live where my crops can grow,
I live where my truth sustains me,
where that is, only I know.

And you say you want to love me,
want to hear all I will tell.
It is there, where I left it,
in the prairie where I dwell.

How Life Slips By

Life is like the weather.
a stormy night,
a gentle breeze,
life slips by in these
like a floating feather.

The Woman in the Mirror

The woman in the mirror frightens me.
She has a dour expression, and she glares.
Her mouth turns down at the edges
The way my grandma's did
And I can't read her face.
I back away.

What must she be thinking
of that smiling young woman,
the one I used to be,
trembling slightly
at the sight of her,
full of apprehension?

A ochenta

Nearing eighty and not miles per hours,
but seconds, minutes, days, weeks, months,
years and decades,
each filled with memories, some fleeting, ephemeral,
some permanent, vying for space in a crowded present.

A *ochenta*, we would say, meaning K's, not miles
as that was as fast as we could go
in the mud rutted streets of our provincial town.
We imagined speed in getting there,
to where we were headed.

Peluchi and I walked arm and arm as girlfriends did
in their after-class strolls through town,
then she turned to me and said, *Quiero ir a ochenta*,
Thinking, I suppose, of our inevitable loss of virginity,
because what followed, said almost dreamily,
was a question:
Do You think Jesus slept with Mary Magdalene?

We were near the Central Market, our bus stop a block away,
the winter sun descending, glare blinding our eyes.
That fleeting moment somehow now revisiting me,
how I then pictured myself
as a Magdalene at the feet of my own savior,
with the urgency of wanting to take
the world by storm, *a ochenta*.

New Directions

Those were the years
I held you close,
looking into the distance
and never looking back.

I think of that today
as I bend down
to fetch a starfish
on the shore,
its radial symmetry
offering new directions.

Death and Mourning

The Business of Living

We'll get down
to the business of living.
First, we'll unload the provisions
and fill up the lair.
We won't prepare table yet.
That will wait.
The fire needs stocking.
The new dry wood brought in.

It will be a long time before
there'll be any sleeping.
Not until she's buried
close beside her kin.

Daffodils

Put away that letter that he never read.
Notify the Navy that our Calvin's dead.

But you can't put away memories
or notify time it must stop.
You can't keep rivers from flowing
or tell the rain not to drop.

Put away his hunting boots and his favorite gun.
Put away his pocketknife that glistened in the sun.

Put away his photographs and his gray knit vest,
hide his body in the earth, time will do the rest.

The clouds, they all have lifted, the sun is shining bright,
And daffodils and buttercups broke through the ground last night.

Oh, we can put away his things and hide his body too,
But, when the daffodils appear, then, what are we to do?

We can always cherish his memory,
our love for him will not stop,
like a river it'll keep on flowing
as flowers spring from rain drops.

When Life Quickens

I have news, I said, in a hurried call to her.
I still gripped the car keys in my hand as
I composed her number.
A light breeze blew through
the open door and followed me in.

News, I have news, I said.
The doctor says
two, maybe three months along,
which explains the nausea.
Mother, are you there?

There was music in
her voice as she responded.
a short, staccato laugh,
relishing the irony,
lead into a tender legato.
There was a slight echo
in the air and the sound
of her voice lingered.

I heard her say,
Now, about my nausea . . .
I got my tests back from Dr. Porter today.
And he says, maybe two, three months,
not long. This type is quick.

The Ledger

The summer I was ten I walked the two blocks
from our house to the hamlet's cemetery,
past headstones of strangers, past
a large square lined with a little fence,
the official gravesite of the family
who lived next door who had three markers
already, and room for three more.

My grandfather's grave was off to one side,
no other kin, no marker, but with a ledger
I could lie on that fit me exactly.

The marble slab felt cool, and after a while
I knew just where to place my hinny so my head
would reach one end and my feet the other.
I would lie there quietly, and let snapshot
memories of my grandfather wash over me.

If I held my arms a bit away from my body
I could reach the edges of the ledger.
Sometimes I would gather my hands under my chin
as I had seen knights do on sarcophagi
in picture books. I never moved my arms
trying to make snow angels. There was no snow.
It was Florida, and besides, it was summer.

The ledger had his name carved into it,
His date of birth, and when he died,
and it was exactly as long as I was tall.

Last Respects

To pay our last respects,
That's why we're going to
My uncle's funeral, Mom said.

My last respects! my heart answered,
how can they be my last?
for till I have memory I'll pay respects
to worked stained, friendly hands,
to twinkling eyes that made
my heart feel glad,
to pleasant tones that earnestly
discussed the latest issues of the state,
to a lazy sort of dress of
working clothes, or clothes for town,
and always with suspenders, red, or brown,
to a heavy form that held me tight and close,
and a voice that cracked and said,
Hello, Sugar while I would pull away
to run across the woods,
or play up in the loft
of the old familiar barn.

These are my respects.
not tears, not words,
just memories of you
I shall respect forever.

1959

A Father's Advice

Drink a glass of water
every time you pee
my father entreated quietly,
ceremoniously,
a week or so before he died.

Why had it taken him
so long to share this
piece of wisdom?

It would have been unseemly,
he said,
to share this with
a child, a young girl, a bride,
a mother - someone else's wife.

He said his advice
had always been
at the tip of his tongue
but he'd refrained.

Until now
when he wanted to pee
in the worst way,
and couldn't.

Jacaranda Blossoms

Death stood by the Jacaranda
and took a deep breath savoring the sweetness
of the purple blooms which mingled in the air,
subdued by Eucalyptus.

Death stood by the Jacaranda
and waited there until you came to me,
came to me one last time, bringing with you
all of the sunlight of the days we'd shared.

Death stood by the Jacaranda
but did not say a word, then leapt between us,
and kissed our cheeks, first your, then mine,
as our eyes met for the last time.

Death stood by the Jacaranda
delivering the words that would be said,
the words we both repeated in farewell.
Then gently, sweetly, counted off the years
as I stayed, transfixed, and you walked away.

Room for Me

She had been religious, given to ecstasy,
To losing her soul and finding it in church.

When she died, I went to services
Thinking now perhaps there would be room for me.

I entered with head bent, overcome
with a sense of presence.
I genuflected. I crossed myself.
I raised my head only to see
her there, still sitting faithfully
In the aisle seat of the second pew.

She had the same voice, the same smile,
the same ecstasy, the same void
willing to be filled.

I sat in my pew and waited.
I sat in my pew and grieved.
I sat, in my pew and waited
For communion could begin.

The Birthday Card

You're depressed, said my friend.
That's so clinical, I thought.
Somehow that word seems
so aloof, so cold, and so unlike
this nauseous sadness,
this churning grief I feel.

Why couldn't we have mourning?

A big black band around my sleeve
to indicate my loss so,
folks who saw it would just look
the other way if they saw tears begin to fall,
or come up to me just to give,
Condolences that's all.

It's depression, say my friends.

I think it's more like reaching for the phone
to tell her all the latest,
and then, remembering,

Or hearing an old hymn at Church she used to love,
and then, remembering.

or walking to the mailbox
and then, remembering,

Today there would have been
a birthday card.

After a Lingering Illness

When Ernesto dies,
I'd like to go to Portugal
and walk along the beach at Estoril.
Its pastel landscape, solid,
yet shimmering from the heat
that rises, African in origin,
angry, moving slowly,
menacingly, toward the West.

I'd run past it unnoticing, focused
only on *Extremadura* or the
Bienteveos of *Jerez.*
Cheers, I'll say once there.
I'll lift my glass and smile.

When Ernesto dies, I'll dress in
black that day, what's left of it,
and for the weeks that follow,
like the widows of Lisbon
walking uphill against the wind,
up crooked little stairs, toward home.

Lovers, Love, and Its Complexities

Our Toy

Let's take a walk today
on some quiet country lane
among the turning leaves
that fell along the way.

Let's laugh in senseless joy
to be two youths in love
pretending that we're Gods
and autumn is our toy.

Bessie's Fern Stand

So, it's come to this.
You in your place, I in mine.
And in my mind, I've drawn
an imaginary line.

I thought it so surprising
that you called me enterprising.
I thought you always hated
my manner of attack.

A fern would help.

I could put it on the fern stand
that had once belonged to Bessie,
the one up in the attic
with her trunks and bric-a-brac.

Yes, I'd put it by a window,
give it water every day,
spray it with a mister,
never thinking what you'd say.

So I drove down to Mother's
and told her what I wanted.
She said, *Honey, you look hungry*
for something that you lack.

Can't say I understand it,
but no need to explain it,
you know that you are welcome
to anything I've got.

You'll find it, disassembled,
in the corner, by the window,
next to Mamma's cedar chest
and Jack's old army cot.

There it was - as I remembered,
just as I had thought.
Thirty years of memories, suspended,
waiting for me. Frozen. Caught.

Bits and Pieces

I want to tumble, tumble, tumble
into your arms, all bits and pieces of me,
colored by experience -
lemon, orange, grape, cherry, licorice.

Tumble, tumble, I want to tumble into your arms
like gum balls tumble, tumble,
tumble out of vending machines.

Tumble, tumble into eager, greedy hands
of someone who has carefully
inserted a coin and waits,
hands cupped.

Carousel

I always thought my turn would come
and you'd be here with me,
The apple trees would be in bloom
as far as we could see.

But that was just a fantasy,
chimerical, strange illusion,
a shaded private garden
with dahlias in profusion.

That orchard that was planted
when you were ten years old
was long ago abandoned,
the land parceled and sold.

And we've been on a journey,
quixotic, side by side,
like ponies in a carousel
on an inverted ride.

Caught Unaware

Sometimes I see you watching me
with a puzzled look on your face,
then the look changes
and tenderness takes its place.

Sometimes I hear you humming
a tune of your own design,
oblivious of those around you
and the fact that you are mine

Chambers of the Heart

Love was synonymous with you.
Your fragrance in a winter morning
brushing against my lips,
waking, arousing,
entering forgotten chambers.

The memory of incense
and the solemn mass,
choirs antiphonally responding,
the tide at sunset
gaining on the shore,
our love was synonymous with this,
and more.

Circles

I remember your loving me,
concentric circles,
a beam of light,
the smell of clean linen
in the still of night.

I remember your holding me
against the softness
of your shirt,
when I ran not away but toward you,
and you kissed away the hurt.

Clear Blue Sky

You thought I was not constant,
you thought I would not stay.
at the first sign of trouble,
you thought I'd go away.

But here I am, undaunted.
I'm what you always wanted,
someone that you could count on
in sunshine or in rain.

Our friends and our relations
scoffed at our expectations,
they said our love would falter,
they said we aimed too high.

But here we are, together,
just sailed through stormy weather,
and all I see before me
is sunlit, clear blue sky.

Cross-cultural French Lessons

I knew then that I would love you,
when I saw you entering the gate,
head bent, watchful, as not to trip
on the crisscross bricks of the path
that led to my door.

Your tall, lean North African body,
a bit bent, and those silly wide suspenders
you wore, the affectation borrowed from
a talk show host you admired,
leaned into me, hand outstretched.

Bon jour, you began, in perfect accented
French without a trace of the Arabic
you spoke at home - that home which
was crowded with stories linked to seven siblings,
their ups, their downs, their kids.

My own *Enfant de Sable*, you would slip
through my fingers, scattered, disappearing,
as ephemeral as the conversations we had,
in French, of course, which I prepared by
reading all I could by Tahar Ben Jelloun.

Department Store Encounter

Our eyes meet, three second, and we look away.
You, walking toward me, I, toward the counter.

The mannequins beckon with their smiles,
their heads askew, their hair too well in place,
their clothes tucked in with safety pins.

And we glance at the mannequins
wishing that in looking back
we'd meet the same impassive eyes.

Instead

Our gaze returns, a second, maybe two,
and there, in the periphery,
each one sees the other disappear,
ut not the feeling that, it could have been.

Devil Chasing

I was running with the devil chasing
making promises I could not keep
and some days was so tired of faking
it took a fifth of whiskey just to fall asleep.

I looked for a lover who was on the level,
I didn't want a lover who would be unkind,
I didn't want sins keeping me from Heaven,
but pure and honest loving was so hard to find!

I'd been searching, searching as I wandered,
could not seem to quench that restless thirst.
Things seemed better for me over yonder
then my dreams like bubbles burst.

Dissonance

You are iambic, and I am dactylic.
You rhyme in couplets, and I use free verse.
communication is seldom idyllic,
except in bed. Guess things could be worse.

Your love is guarded while I love you freely,
but your love is steady while I love in spurts.
I tease you; I leave you, and sometimes deceive you,
and then I'm surprised when you tell me it hurts.

So, we go on and we hurt one another,
not even alike in the weapons we use.
Your silence is piercing, my rhetoric deafening,
and neither one happy cause both of us lose.

Do I Dare?

To Hank

Standing on the vertiginous
edge of possibility,
I glance back and see you there,
the last precious rays of light
playing leapfrog with your hair.

What does the night bring,
if not the morning?
I stand on the edge.
You wait behind,
but sound no warning.

The sun's long rays of light
like giant fingers
tussle through your hair.
My heart expands and shrinks.
Do I leap? Do I dare?

Dusk

You're the one I run to. He don't mind.
You're the one who's never been unkind.
You're the one safe harbor at my shore.
You're the one who's never closed the door.

You're the one I talk to when I'm low,
and when you're gone, My God, I miss you so.
To you my sins and sorrows I confess,
for you're the one I really love, I guess.

You're the one who's always been my friend.
With you I never needed to pretend.
I've loved you for so long, for half my life,
almost as long as I have been his wife.

Don't laugh at me, at my ideas don't scoff.
I don't know where you start and I leave off.
With you my past and future seem to meet;
I try but find it hard to be discrete.

Sometimes we don't agree, and I feel lost.
I used to buy you back at any cost,
with time I saw my strategy was sin,
for pride, not love, was what made me give in.

The issues multiply but seem unreal.
It's doubtful they reflect the way we feel,
A consequence of friendship and of lust,
we're lost in a strange village, and it's dusk.

Edge of the Sunset

I will go to the edge of the sunset
where the day begins again,
where light melts away to nothingness,
to the fragrance of your skin.

I will wear a suit of blue linen,
neatly pressed and creased just right.
I will go to the edge of the desert,
and patiently wait the night.

Ego Trip

You were on an ego trip,
I went along for the ride.
You did all the driving,
I sat on the passenger's side.

I asked, *where are you going?*
You said you did not know,
so, I pulled out my road map
and showed you where to go.

We did not take the main roads
for they all charged a toll.
But all that circumspection
has cost us both our soul.

First Love

Because we were so young that spring,
you only took my hand,
and talked of gentle, simple things,
of things I'd understand.

We walked along the countryside,
through twisted road and lea,
and gathered flowers that grew wild,
and laughed so happily!

You were fourteen and I thirteen,
and we were both so young
that neither you nor I suspected
our song would go unsung.

And hand and hand we walked and walked,
I guess we walked for miles
through country roads and grassy downs,
how happy were our smiles!

We were so gay and innocent
that day in early spring,
we chanted rhymes we knew by heart,
and laughed at everything.

We were so happy that spring day,
so innocent and free!
Now, sometimes, I ask myself
if you remember me.

Fitful Sleep

I don't care if there's someone else.
Don't want to hear about it.
There's been talk you love us both,
as for me, I would not doubt it.

Sometimes when you're sound asleep
you talk while you are dreaming.
I pretend that I don't hear
the things that you are scheming.

The name you call is not my own,
can't say it does not hurt.
Sometimes it isn't good, I think,
to be all that alert.

Getting There

Yes, I will say yes to the morning.
Yes, I will say yes to the night.
Yes, I can feel your longing
to bathe my body with delight.

Yes, I can hear the murmur
of your heartbeat as it sounds
for the depth of our shared passion
and the station where we're bound.

We're both travelers in a journey
at the crossroads of our lives,
bees among the orange blossoms
darting in and out of hives

Lonely, hurting, solitary,
caught in an unending flight
longing to say yes to mourning,
longing to say yes to night.

Getting to Know You

I don't want to know your secrets
the ones you have savored
and guarded for years
remembering every detail, every nuance
as though they were flash frozen,
the ones you have kept at safe distance,
those you knew you would never reveal.

I don't want to know your secrets,
the ones you have polished
and rehearsed to reveal
at just the right moment,
the ones you use as weapons,
as crutches,
as shields.

I want to know you, the person
who stands before me,
vulnerable, complicated,
wanting to be loved.

The Grass is Greener

Wish I knew how to tell you, but I really just don't know.
It's a feeling I've been having and each day I watch it grow.

That grass out there gets greener each time you make me blue,
and it's getting ever harder for me, Baby, to stay true.

If you took the time to notice you would recognize the signs,
that I'm growing, that I'm changing. Wish you'd read between the
lines.

Ever since we've been together, you have toyed with my heart,
but you never once considered it was driving us apart.

I've been trying hard to please you, but you just don't seem to care,
and it takes all that is in me not to sink into despair.

Memories of good times together is what keeps me hanging on
but I'm running out of memories. All the happy times are gone.

Yes, the grass out there got greener each time you made me blue.
Babe, you made it oh, so easy just to say goodbye to you.

Halcyon Days

Those were the peaceful years. The wind
would blow past on its way to Tennessee,
and we would lie there, under the tin roof
listening to its cadence.

Outside our bedroom the plumb tree flowered,
the petals falling covering the grass with white.

We waited. Knowing that fruit would come,
growing, plumping up, and all the while
we'd think of the jam we'd make in copper pots.

The wind blew past, the rain pelting,
the limbs heavy with fruit,
giving, touching the ground.
You and I listening, holding hands.

Running to the Beat of Rocky Top

I run. I watch a band of ducks
in parabolic flight
head for the distant lake.

I run. I feel my strength returning,
your gentle healing love
guides every step I take.

I run. I listen to my Walkman
syllabicate *Rocky Top,*
and fall in tandem with the beat.

I run. Motion is forward, strong,
closer, ever closer to the place
where soul and body meet.

I run. Sweat begins to trickle
down my face. It stings. Effort
is salty, real, something I can taste.

I run. The wind rustles, and swirls,
and bends, and curves as my legs
cut through fast, but without haste.

Imaginings

It would be sweet with you, bubbly,
A *kir royal*,
sweet currant syrup and champagne
drunk in a chamber of my heart
where no other man has lain.

I like a man like you,
who cuts straight to the chase,
a man for whom I'd drop my veil
of tulle and lace.

The stories we would tell
each other, you and I!
First, we'd laugh,
we'd giggle,
we'd convulse,
then cry.

Intertwined

I will step into the light
and take your hand.
Together we will walk
along the strand,

together we will go
into the darkening night
and sleep until we wake,
together, intertwined.

Just a Day

And so, you were my lover for just one day.
I don't think that I would have it any other way.

Just a day. That is all. And that is fine.
But, for just that day, you were mine. All mine.

That is all I wanted. That is all I got.
Some things, I think, are better when they're not

Lemon Light

The light was lemon yellow, and the breeze felt cool.
We had a picnic lunch beside a Moorish pool,
and talked about the gypsies we met on the way
up to Castel San Jorge that September day.

The sailboats in the harbor looked like little toys
left out on a pond by naughty little boys,
and we could see for miles the Portuguese fine coast
from that old Moorish castle which is Lisbon's boast.

Kathryn picked an olive from a nearby tree,
said, *Now we have hors d'oeuvres*, and then laughed merrily.
We both joined in the laughter as we sipped our port
and finished up our picnic in the Moorish court.

And though ten years have passed that day's still on my mind.
I felt so close to you, our hearts were so entwined,
that now September breezes fill my life with songs
And lemon light reminds me where my heart belongs.

Lessons

I've learned not to hitch my chariot to a shooting star.
I've learned not to yell "come get me!"
Until you know where you are.

I've learned sometimes three is company
and two's a crowd.

I've learned to lie there playing possum
with sunshine and clouds.

The Letter on the Shelf

I want things to be like they were before,
this time all grown up and knowing the score
for there's one thing I've learned since I left your side,
it's sure hard to live with secrets to hide.

Oh, when we fell in love, I was just a child.
I did some rash things, let my feelings run wild,
and all of the trust that you had in me
died on that day I begged to be free.

I want things to be like they were before,
this time all grown up and knowing the score
for there's one thing I've learned since I left your side,
when I said I don't care, I must have just lied.

So, I'm coming home if you'll take me back
cause, Baby, I've found what I thought I lack.
like that letter of Poe's sitting on the shelf,
it was there all along, just inside myself.

Love Realized

My soul sang once with sadden tones
of unrequited love
and found no trouble to express
the love that I dreamed of.

But now love is reality
and I can't write a line!
for how could I express in rhyme
a love as deep as mine?

Lovers

I thought we would be lovers, but it was not to be,
for lovers are like rivers that empty out to sea.

And we are like two palm trees growing side by side,
rigid, and yet yielding to the wind and tide.

I thought we would be lovers, but it was not to be,
for lovers are like instruments that play a symphony.

And we are like the swallows returning to the plain,
all decked out in morning coats, resting in the rain.

I thought we would be lovers, but it was not to be,
for we are standing firm instead of blowing free!

We'll never be one body, we'll never be one sound,
for each of us to others by broken vows is bound.

Missing You

I climbed a hill the other day
and lay there resting on the clay,
watching birds and languid flight
soar from day into the night.

I watched them till all light had fled
into night's still, lazy bed
and wondered in my loneliness
if they too missed your warm embrace.

No Regrets

You're all that matters now, the rest I can forget.
You're my present. You're my future.
There's no past; there's no regret.

When I was much younger, aloof, and so proud,
I didn't want anyone hanging around.
But now I am older, and old friends are few,
I know I can't make it, alone, without you.

So, please treat me gently, don't shout and don't pound.
Don't make me hide feelings or my longings bound.
I want a tomorrow; I want to look back
on what came before you but stay on the track.

Not Enough

They didn't say a word. No words were needed.
There once had been a flood of love
but the waters had receded.

They walked along the sidewalk,
holding hands, looking ahead,
he to the right, she to the left.

She thought about the day
They had spent in Fontainbleu.

He thought about the projects
That he still had to do.

She thought about the babies,
How different each had been.

He thought about the patients he had seen.

She thought about how nice the park looked in the fall.

He thought about how terrible he'd felt about that call.

Not enough time, not enough, they thought.
Not enough time, not enough

On the Beach

I am going to savor this one
for I know it is my last.
A new beginning, and I wonder,
how many new beginnings
have there been in recent past?

Changes, imperceptibly
sneaking into consciousness!
Oh, I know that they are happening,
I'm aware, more or less.
Stealthily, slowly, cataclysmic,
somehow ever out of reach.

But this time
I know it's different.
You're there waiting for me,
on the beach.

One Night Stand in Normandy

He sat perched on the windowsill,
smoking a cigarette, and,
at the sight of him, she laughed.

Tu blagues, quoi, he said.

He had made love to her, slowly, silently, leisurely,
and had never said a word.
Just as silently, she had allowed herself
to come into his arms, aware, by then,
that he had stalked and watched her
to learn by heart the measures needed
to reach that night.

And now he sat looking out the window
which opened to a Norman summer sky
still tinged with light.

From there, she knew, he could see Cambridge,
and Senegal was quite forgotten
as the rooftops of Brooklyn
disappeared from sight.

Our Life

We entered a difficult age
Of uncertainties, disappointments
And regrets.

So sure that
We'd found ourselves at last,
as we had lost each other.

Reality changed hues,
Intensities, and depths,
and rose, like bubbles

made of colored soap perfumed, and stolen from
that get-away hotel where we had tried,
just one last time, to get it all together,

Up to the ceiling
of our life.

Parting Words

Your words echoed off the canyons of memory,
ricocheting like sunshine bounces off glass buildings
in the city.

Your words were brilliant, and they blinded me.
They were songs of deafening rhythms that
gripped my heart.

What did you say? Do you remember?
solid words, well enunciated, well meaning,
kind.

They fell like thunder rolls off lightening
after the sky has extinguished
its light.

I thought about it - what you'd just uttered -
you know, it's funny, you were right,
so right.

Promises

Promises made, promises broken,
give me a kiss, I need a token.
I need to know our love will last.
I need to break away from the past.

Jackson, Jackson, on the run,
Come on home and have some fun!
You've been gone for seven hours.
You better have a bunch of flowers

before you come knocking at my door.
Look at the time, it's ten till four.
Horseman, horseman, pull at the rein!
Come on home, let's raise some Cain!
Life was made for celebration,
you work too hard, take a vacation!

Joyful! Joyful! Sound the drum!
Don't be glum, don't be ho-hum!
Come on home, make love to your wife,
Can't you see you're the love of her life?

Stars they shine so clear at dawn,
then, so soon, so soon are gone,
like fears that in the dark shine bright
then disappear when given light.

Reflecting on Times Past

We talked all night
and into the following morning.
We were lovers,
angry and bruised,
wanting to be friends.
And it is your eyes that I remember,
piercing through the darkness.
They were cold and still.

That was the year you began,
time and again,
as I shivered.
That was the time,
Or was it ...
No, there were so many
So many times ...
Hard to keep them apart.

Images emerged in
those cold, hard eyes -
reflections of what you saw
as you had seen me.
There I was, dancing in your eyes
through all those years
through all those times.

No longer trapped
on the other side
of my reflection.

Seduction

Shall I be a piece of fiction?
contrive a middle, beginning, and an end?
I can be, oh, so convincing
you would swear I don't pretend.

I can tell what would intrigue you
long enough to keep you here.
I know what to state succinctly,
and just what to keep unclear.

And whatever I will tell you
you will think about for years
trying to re-group the sequence
of what walked you through your fears.

Silent Partners

We run the same miles, you, and I,
a day and a half apart.
you run ahead, I run behind,
enjoying the solitude of your head-start.

I run faster trying to catch up and think.
Our shadows meet and then run side by side.
Janus, I think, full-bodied Janus, I think.
Full-bodied, just like the Beaujolais I drink.

I am pondering the question
you've just asked yourself,
but the answer eludes me,
running past, silently.

Sonnet

Oh, must you blame me if I sing my thoughts?
I am a poet, why should that be wrong?
Or must you curse me just because I caught
a fleeting thought and turned it into song?
Oh, how I've wept because of you, my dear,
when just by chance a thought came to my mind
that made me sing a lyric soft and clear,
but your reproach made it to be confined.
Yet I must sing of you and of our love,
and also of the rain, and winds, and leas,
and gentle, tiny birds that fly above
the chimney tops and nestle in the trees,
and of the sunshine and the morning dew,
and of the universe, and God, and you.

Steering through Uncharted Waters

Sailing through uncharted waters,
oh, good Captain do you see
anything that might detain us
in our passion to be free?

I am waiting to be guided
by the stars of a clear night
I am waiting for good weather,
for conditions to be right.

Oh, good Captain, my dear Captain,
climb the mast that you might see,
for your limbs are strong and steady,
leave the steering up to me.

I have with me the ship's journals
I'll consult them while I steer
oh, we've traveled such a distance
our port surely must be near.

Stranger

Why did you leave me?
Where did you go?
What prompted the journey?
When did you return?
How long has it been
since you've knocked at my door?
Tell me. Tell me all that,
Tell me more.

Summer Rain

Purple thistles by the lane
welcomed us that day,
and pink wild roses blushed and smiled
when're we looked their way.

We walked in silence, you, and I,
but now and then we'd laugh
to see the ducklings in the pond,
or some young awkward calf.

And when we stopped beside the rill
you kissed me with a sigh,
and whispered words unsaid before
to which I answered "aye".

We lingered on till stars appeared
in that old country lane,
and oh, the night that greeted us
had not a sign of rain.

The stars were bright, the moon was full,
as our hearts were of love,
and heaven seemed to smile at us
and bless us from above.

But then a sudden summer rain
that took us by surprise
splashed silent tears on my face
and seemed to cool your sighs.

Now once again the summer rain
falls swiftly on the lea
as echoes to my useless tears,
and cries, come back to me!

Tabouleh

to Hank

There's a Middle Eastern food store on highway Ninety-Two
and that's where I go shopping when nothing else will do.

The sweetness of their apricots, the crispness of their bread,
the fragrance of their feta, go right up to my head.

Their almonds and their lentils, their coriander seeds
peek out of canvas bags and seem to fill my needs.

I sample the tabouleh, the nuts, the baklava.
I'm happy; I'm restored, then rush back where you are.

Taken for Granted

Thinking of you is
such an easy feeling.
The mornings that we share
are full of sunshine.

The afternoons slip by
pushed by gentle breezes
that roll over the hills and plains
of our memories.

Somnambulist, the two of us,
each speaks, each calling out.
And yet, like sleepwalkers,
we smile at one another
and answer the questions
that by morning
we refuse to acknowledge.

Purple

We will create a new reality,
strong and supple,
equal parts of blue and red -
the color purple.

You will bring the sunshine,
I will bring the rain,
and there will be crops,
again.

The Glockenspiel

I see you, in my mind's eye, a hundred yards away.
It feels, I want to tell you, as it were yesterday.

You're standing by the elm tree, your hat is in your hand,
upstairs the wine is chilling, I'm listening to The Band.

The glockenspiel is sounding the hour to begin,
but Munich seems as distant as snow covered Berlin.

I call to you. You hear me and toss your hat up high
then run ahead to catch it as it falls from the sky.

What you held was so precious, so secret, and so fine,
so durable, so supple, so yours, I made it mine.

The Look

A wave
of self-loading
had washed over me.

I had walked away.
I had left
not running away,
not running toward,
but to gain space,
to stand my ground.

And there I stood.
not triumphant
nor defeated,
but suspended
without a past
that followed me
or a future,
waiting.

Then you looked
at me.
and your insouciant glee,
conspiratorial in its promise,
seemed to beckon.

The Nameless Lover

I always had a nameless longing,
my heart had always held a space
reserved for a young nameless lover
I'd recognize when face to face.

He came to me; he was the morning.
He came to me; I was mid-day.
He came to me; love gave no warning.
Oh, don't take Daniel, Daniel away.

Trapped

Come back here, he yelled,
but she kept walking,
and both wondering
just how far she'd go
before she returned,
because she always did.

There was a shiver,
almost audible,
as one wondered in hope,
and one in panic.

Unbridled Passion

Six stallions thundered down the mountain
galloping toward the dunes bellow.
Six stallions white, and chestnut, dappled,
their riders, absent, had let them go.

Their course was rhythmic, their course was steady,
it was elliptical to keep them straight,
lest they should falter, lest they should tumble
in their descent and miss the gate.

West Wing

I was one of the loves of Yousef,
the one who lived in the West Wing,
and each fortnight before daybreak
his sweet song to me he'd sing.

I was a tree in his private garden,
of almond, apricot, and peach.
And each fortnight before daybreak,
he gathered what was within reach.

Stories

Speaking the Same Language

Mother learned French because she planned to be a missionary in the Middle East, but her life got sidetracked by World War II. Instead of going to Syria, the Southern Baptist Missionary Board sent her and my father to Spanish-speaking Argentina where I was born a year after their arrival. By the time I was old enough to talk to her about those early years as a misplaced Alabamian in the Buenos Aires of 1940s, she was fluent in Spanish and spoke it with no trace of English or French, and it was difficult for me to imagine her at a loss for words in any language. She was extraordinary.

"But what did you *do* about not being able to speak Spanish?" I insisted, eager to hear the details of how she went about learning to speak so perfectly.

"I went to the *Berlitz* school for a year," she said, then demurred a little and added, "you see, I also had Marie."

Marie was my mother's Rosetta Stone. A French national, she had been widowed soon after her arrival in Argentina, and when her funds began to run low, she became a mother's helper.

"So, you see, my French came in handy after all," Mother said, for it was in French that she and Marie spoke.

There was never any question about what language I would speak. Argentina was my native country and Spanish was my native tongue. Sometime in the distant future, I would "return" to the English-speaking world, but that language belonged to my parents. It was the language of lullabies, bedtime stories, and later, after-school private lessons with a succession of British tutors.

When I was a teenager, my family returned to live in the United States. I was fairly fluent in English, although I spoke it haltingly and with a detectable Spanish accent, but Marie's French had long since been forgotten. About all, I could remember was a lullaby that began "*Fait Do-do . . .*" and sounded a little like "Twinkle, Twinkle Little Star." However, as years went by, I felt my case was something akin to orphans separated from their siblings and placed in foster homes who have vague memories of their former lives and the nagging feeling that they have brothers and sisters somewhere. There was a linguistic vacuum in my life, a sense of loss, a sadness I could not explain.

As I grew older, the role English and Spanish played in my life underwent a reversal. Growing up, in South America, English made only occasional intrusions into my life. In the United States, I put Spanish aside. My brother and sister, who were younger, dropped it altogether. But I did not and neither did my mother. She became a language teacher and taught Spanish for the next twenty years. I followed in her footsteps. My career, however, was short-lived— abandoned with the demands of bringing up children.

Mother died in my mid thirties, a few months after the birth of my fourth child, whom I named Julia, in her honor. I was disconsolate. She was my best if most distant friend. We had not lived near each other since my leaving home for college, but we were frequently in touch. She was not only my mother, but she was also my father-confessor. We had an ongoing private joke. When she sensed I was troubled, she asked, "Well, do you need help on sins of *commission* or sins of *omission*?" then laughed to let me know that I should lighten up.

Without her to turn to my "sins" were ever before me, for any chance of atonement had been buried along with her. And that was not the only problem. My brother was divorcing, my sister was moving to the midwest, and my father had been diagnosed as having cancer. And he had begun to peek out of his closet. I had never felt so alone.

I suppose that is why I began humming to myself, whistling in the dark, as it were, to keep myself company. First, it was lullabies, the ones Mother and Marie had sung to me, then it was ballads I made up about my life. It was during the late seventies, and we were the thirty-somethings. Most of my friends were divorcing, unhappy, unfulfilled, or restless. Everywhere I looked there was betrayal, denial, and a mad rush to get there. But get where? Where was everybody rushing off to? Everyone seemed to be watching the pitcher, stealing bases. I felt like the batter, alone at the plate.

For me, those years were "the best of times and the worst of times," and just as destructive and revolutionary. To cope with all the changes, I became a regular Madame Defarge. But instead of incorporating my little secrets into knitting patterns, I made up ballads. At first, the ballads were poems that then morphed into songs with tunes of their own. When I ran out of things to write about, I scanned the newspaper looking for stories as gothic as the ones unfolding around me and made songs out of them too. After a couple of years of writing ballads, and putting some of my poems into songs, decided to see if I could get someone to make lead sheets out of them for me. I contacted the music association. That's how I met Lenny.

Lenny had been a music major in college and was now doing a little bit of carpentry to make ends meet. Music was what he lived and breathed, but gigs were hard to come by for his little rock band, so he took on any musical project he could find, not that they were plentiful in a town like this. He would be glad to be of service, he said.

I'd never known anyone like him. He approached life with disarming candor and insouciance. He was part conjurer, part priest, and part psychiatrist, but had none of their heaviness, only their perception and a strange ability to dispense absolution.

I was astounded by his musical ability. He could hear my songs on tape, and without any instruments, write a lead sheet for them on the kitchen table of his little shabby midtown apartment where an opened box of breakfast cereal sat on the counter along with a half-empty can of cat food, a scribble pad full of numbers he had written down for possible gigs, and the dirty clothes his stepson had taken off the night before. That's where we would meet, from time to time, in his kitchen, and it always looked pretty much the same. Until one day, I came in, and everything had been cleaned off, even the scribble pad because Lenny had declared bankruptcy, and he was not taking any calls. His wife had left him taking the kid and the cats. Lenny was skipping breakfast.

The first time I went to his apartment, he ushered me into the kitchen and motioned me to sit down at the little table. He took off his glasses, became very serious, and tapped the tabletop with his fingers. "We are going to have to have a love affair; that is how close we will have to be because if not, we can't work together," he said, and gave me a wry smile. He put his glasses back on and said, "But you understand what I mean by a love affair, *of course*, no sex. What I mean is, we are going to have to get so close that we can end each other's sentences." And we did. We worked comfortably together in an accepting, easygoing way. Although I had as much trouble accepting his poverty, which I felt was the direct result of his inertia, as he had accepting my drive and prolific output. As we worked through the songs, he'd ask me what had prompted my lyrics and listened patiently to my stories. From the lyrics, and from the mournful tunes of some of the songs, it was easy to guess that I was, as they say in Nashville, hurting—hurting bad. But Lenny never did say anything about that, nor asked me any subliminal questions that might have revealed what I wasn't telling. Instead, he said to me one day, "Why don't you write me a couple of kid songs sometime. Maybe even one or two in Spanish."

A few months later, as we worked in his kitchen, he took off his glasses and started tapping *The William Tell Overture* on the tabletop. I could tell he was nervous, and I braced myself a little. It wasn't like Lenny to make pronouncements, but I figured whatever was on his mind must have been important because soon he began to mark time with his foot.

"Look, ah, your ballads are great," he said. "But I've been thinking . . . the personal is too personal, and the stuff you took out of the newspapers could land you in court with a libel suit. Kids. Now, that's the direction you need to go. You could volunteer in the schools and teach Spanish with songs. Let's drop the ballads for a while and concentrate on kids."

I took his advice, quit writing ballads, and began writing bilingual children's songs. By that time, I was playing piano rather well and jotting down my own compositions. I'd studied Lenny's lead sheets enough to know how to do that, too, so as I got more involved in writing music for children, I called on him less and less. Then in Paris, last winter, something reminded me of Lenny, and I realized that it had been years since he'd crossed my mind.

I'd written all those songs about my own kids, that's what Lenny said made them so good, but now the children were grown, and I had time on my hands. The stack of lyrics and lead sheets were stored in a hatbox on the top shelf of my closet—my interest in music had been put aside and replaced with language study. For the past few years, I had been studying French.

Marie's lullabies had always haunted me. Most of my life, the vague memories of my mother's French conversations with her felt like an amputee's missing limbs. When I began to learn French, I experienced a feeling of calm and joy that was difficult to explain. I felt whole, at home. But the leap from half-forgotten lullabies and baby talk to fluency had not been easy, it had been hard work.

After several false tries and almost giving up the idea of trying to attain fluency, I found a language school in the sixteenth *arrondissement* of Paris that was a perfect fit. It was possible to attend it for a week or two at a time and "plug in" at various levels of proficiency as I advanced in my language learning. My goal was to visit the school from time to time until I could participate in *L'Express*, a current events class opened only to advanced students.

I reached a point in my studies where I felt I was ready to enter the class and decided to challenge myself by beginning the year with a two-week stint in Paris. To my delight, I found that what a Parisian January lacked in daylight hours and *Jardin Fleuris*, it more than made up in the scarcity of foreigners. The atmosphere both in the city itself and the school was easygoing, friendly, and relaxed.

The current events class was small and multinational. There were only three of us—Anders, a Swedish military attaché; Ursula, a

Swiss bank employee; and I. Our teacher was Dominique, whom we christened "La Belle France." Each day, we read the news magazine *L'Express* and discussed French current events seen through the prism that we were, a Swiss, Swedish, American trio. I loved to see our diverse composite parts coming together. By the end of the first week, we in complete harmony.

It was not unusual for the students to get together after class to gossip a bit about the school and compare notes. One of the things we all had in common was our love of foreign languages, and most of us had traveled in each other's countries. The day before my departure, Anders said, "I don't have too much time tonight because there is a meeting at the embassy I have to attend, but I would love to squeeze in dinner with you. You pick the place. You know Paris better than I do."

It would be nice to have dinner with Anders, I thought. He had spent a summer in Mississippi, and I knew he was eager to reminisce about it. I accepted his invitation. Though he was Swedish and I was American, we would go Dutch.

I asked him if he knew the Notre-Dame area to which he replied, *"bien sûr!"* and looked a little hurt that I would have asked such a question. *But did he know about the other island next to it?*

"No," he said, he didn't even realize Notre-Dame was on an island. "What other island?"

"Isle St. Louis," I said, "lovely little place with only one main street running through it. Lots of restaurants. I have one in mind I think you'll like, but if for some reason it doesn't appeal to you, there's *Le Sergent's Recruteur* or *Nos Ancêtres les Gaulois* down the street. Good tourist places, both."

"French? You sure it's French? Seems Paris is overrun with Thai and Italian places. I haven't had a French meal yet."

I assured him that it would be French. I was right in my opinion of Anders. He was exacting.

"But are you sure?" he insisted, and I began to get exasperated.

"Meet me at the Hôtel de Ville metro stop. Seven-ish. No need to break your neck. If you can't make it on time, I'll people watch."

A few minutes past seven, a harried Anders appeared as if out of nowhere. He was in full uniform. He clicked his heels and greeted me with an exaggerated mock salute. "This is no joke, so stop laughing. I had no time to change after the embassy. I don't cut that funny a figure, do I?"

"It isn't that. It's something I was not expecting. Military attaché, you said, but I didn't think . . ." my voice trailed off as he took my arm, and we began walking toward the bridge. I felt as though I had my own private bodyguard.

Over dinner, we talked about what Anders's little boys would do in Paris about learning French and how they would keep up with their Swedish. "Did you know there is a Swedish center in the *Marais*, a few blocks from here?" I said, trying to be helpful. He said yes, he knew. He'd already enrolled the boys in an after-school program, and I gathered from the conversation that ensued, he had also taken care of all the rest of the details of getting his family resettled. His apartment was in the 17th *arrondissement*. "Good school district," he told me, but what had really sold him on it was that it was so convenient, he was sure his wife would love it. Plenty of shops all around it, even a post office on the corner. It would make her transition after the move from Sweden with the boys so much easier. He had even managed to talk the landlord into having the apartment repapered and change the draperies to make it more livable. Anders smiled smugly and winked at me as he told me of that little coup.

"Now, dear heart, I am off for a long weekend of skiing before the wife and kiddies arrive Tuesday. No need to worry about old Anders, I've got it all under control." He reached across the table and patted my arm in an avuncular way.

That year, January had begun with record cold but had thawed out to temperatures as balmy as any spring. After dinner, we decided to take advantage of the warm weather and walk back to my hotel on the 7th skirting the Seine. But we overshot a bit for midnight caught us at the Alexandre III bridge just as the lights went out on the *Esplanade des Invalides,* and Anders began to get anxious. He thought that because of the hour he might miss his metro connection.

Then where would he be? He said, "I hate to do this to you, a bit ungracious and all, but I think you'll be all right the rest of the way alone." He pecked me on the cheek, gave me another little mock salute, and hurried off with an air of military march to his step.

As I stood alone on the bridge, a little shiver ran through me. Anders's conversation had reminded me of my parents, half a world and half a century away, setting up housekeeping far away from home, learning a new language, and worrying about how they would manage to bring up their children bilingual.

I liked the way Anders and I had chatted at the restaurant. It had been in an easy, uncomplicated way—about his kids, settling in, his new life in France, and about his summer as an exchange student in Biloxi. And, as we talked, we shifted back and forth from English to French, throwing in an occasional Spanish or Swedish expression, depending on the story. That was the way Lenny and I used to write, trying out different chords until we came up with one that fit the spirit of the song.

As I walked across the Alexander III bridge which moments ago had been flooded with light and now stood dimly backlit by the moon reflecting on the water of the Seine, I thought about the bridges in my life. My parents had used French as a bridge to help them settle into a new country and had relied on Marie. But what means had I used to help me settle into new realities? When I began to tumble into adulthood and saw my life redefine itself in the aftermath of my mother's death, I rearranged the chaos that overwhelmed me into neat little quatrains to make it manageable. Humming my ballads helped me keep in step with life. But I had only been marking time. I had gone through life haunted by Mother's lullabies, searching for the meaning behind the words of a language I did not understand.

I reached the end of the bridge keeping my eye on the Eiffel Tower, for I was now in the 7th *arrondissement*, headed back to my hotel on rue Amélie. I felt tired and sleepy and began to whistle *Fait Do-Do* . . . which I now know meant, *Go to sleep* . . . in French baby talk. It was then that I thought about Lenny and those years that surrounded his memory. Why had I thought of him? Had it been the lullaby, or was there some connection between him and Anders? My mind searched for some random similarity between such disparate characters. They were about the same height and had more or less the same coloring, and both had a way of starting a sentence as though they had thought about what they were going to say before they said it. And another thing—Lenny's kitchen table was about the size of the one at the restaurant, and the surroundings just as cluttered. Maybe that was it.

Or was it that with each of them there had been that special camaraderie born from speaking the same language?

The Point

I think of little stories to tell you,
conclusions drawn carefully
with well sharpened pencils.
little stories with preludes retold s morals
drawing us closer to the point.

Les Tisanes d'Automne

The stories came later, after the taste of
mint, verbena, and lemon balm
had satisfied their thirst,
their affairs in order, the front stoop swept.

Late afternoon came early that time of year
and the sapling cut down during the renovation
had had time to season. It made good kindling.

They would open the flue, build a fire with the wood
stacked in neat piles next to the back door,
and say nothing at first, in anticipation of winter.

The Defrocked Priest

Her soul was possessed by an evil spirit
who ruled her life for years.
She went to the priest to make her confession,
could hardly speak for the tears.
Her soul was troubled, she could not sleep,
she'd wake in fright and weep,
yet, for her pain there was no cause,
against her sins no laws.

And she cried, *Absolution, absolution!*
Father, Father, what's the solution?
Monstrous riddles with frightening answers
grow and sicken me like cancer.

The priest reached down and touched her shoulder,
tried to comfort her, to hold her.
It was then that he could feel
The spirit, there, cold and real.

He looked at her, her tear-filled eyes,
said, *Child, oh, child, you stop those lies!*
What you are saying I've heard before.
And I can't take it anymore.

Absolution, absolution!
I'm so tired of those solutions,
This priest's life has become slow death
I take with every breath.

She left his office without a word.
He'd been her final hope.
She'd tried to warn him of a great evil,
but he'd misjudged its scope.

She thought it better to stay away
and have some time to think,
Then she went back the Sunday next
and drank the thrice blessed drink.

What she found there was Absolution.
Truth for her, was the one solution.
But in turning back the clock,
The priest had lost his frock.

For Sale

Everybody has a story, everybody has a tale,
and at one time or another everybody is for sale

Yes, the whore will sell her body and she'll charge you for her time.
Plenty others do the same thing, just you listen to my rhymes.

Oh, the priest will sell salvation, and the doctor sell you health,
and the conman sell you false hope with his promises of wealth.

Heard a German told a story about a man who sold his soul,
and he sold it to the Devil just to keep from getting old.

So if you think that you're different, sell yourself you never could,
well, my friend, you haven't listened, or you have misunderstood.

For the moral of the story, yes, the message in the tale
Is that some time or another, everybody is for sale.

Alphabet Pasta

Adam, Benjamin, Charles, David, Edward, and Frank
went out walking one day, and never, never came back.

Oh, horrors, how could that be? They only went to the store.
Make up another verse and tell us, tell us some more.

Gigi, Heather, and Irm, Janet, Katie, and Lu
all went out after them, now they have disappeared, too.

Martin, Otto, and Nick, Pat, and Quentin, and Sam,
said *Let's get Russell and Ted or we'll be in the same jam!*

Terry, Ursula, Vern, Wanda, Xavier, and Zane
got Yolanda to help, but never came back again.

Oh, stop! I've finally caught on! C'est tout, genug, enough, basta!
You've just been putting us on, it's only alphabet pasta

Freddie

Freddie was an elephant who lived quite near the sea
with his mother and his father. A family of three.
Freddie's mother was quite worried, yes, she was quite dismayed!
You see, Freddie was so shy that he seldom ever played.

He was timid with the fishes swimming in the sea!
He was timid with the monkeys swinging in the trees!
He was timid with the sand-crabs basking in the sun!
Freddie was so timid that he never had much fun.

One day Freddie's mother said, "Make room for just one more,
this family of three will be a family of four!
Freddie's mother was quite happy! Yes, she was oh, so proud!
You see soon a baby brother was born in the compound.

And the news soon reached the fishes swimming in the sea.
And the news soon reached the monkeys swinging in the trees.
And the news soon reached the sand-crabs basking in the sun,
and they wondered if the brother would be different and have fun.

Freddie's brother sure was different, everyone said, "My, oh, my!"
You see, he was so outgoing, and he wasn't a bit shy.
And a change came over Freddie when his brother and he played.
Freddie soon became so friendly, everybody was amazed!

He made friends with all the fishes swimming in the sea.
He made friends with all the monkeys swinging in the trees.
He made friends with all the sand-crabs basking in the sun.
Oh, yes, Freddie was so different he was always having fun.

Good Luck Charms for Sale

The sign says *Good Luck Charms for Sale*.
That's just whom I must see.
Tomorrow is your christening day, so be expecting me!
Now, I'm off to see the Gypsy and ask about your fate.
I dreamed about a train last night—the boxcars numbered eight.
The first car was a number one, and then there was a three.
That may not mean that much to you, but it sure frightened me!
For the numbers on those boxcars was the date that you were born,
But talking 'bout those matters has always brought me scorn.

Some people say I'm crazy - I think I'm just insane.
these damn fool premonitions have brought me nothing but pain.
Sometimes the feelings linger, and then they just don't last.
Sometimes they're of the future, sometimes they're of the past.
I've got to be real careful about what I say and do,
Like making wild predictions for fear they will come true.

Now I'm going to see that Gypsy and get some good advice
Cause when I saw that train derail my heart, it turned to ice.
The people came from nearby towns and worked all through the night
and when that train was up again, I read from left to right.
The numbers on those boxcars, they did not look the same,
instead, I saw eight letters, and they spelled out name.

Innocence and Goodness

Lost it at the bell tower when she was twelve years old.
He told her, *don't tell, girl!* so she never told.
Mama, it would have killed her! Papa, he wouldn't cared,
So, she never told them, she just never dared.

Sunday School was over, and she was going home.
He came quoting Scripture, said she should learn some.
He had a lot to teach her, she had a lot to learn,
And as he came closer, fire within her burned.

He said, Job had Tribulations, young David was a king.
Solomon had wisdom and did prodigious things.
Wrote a book so sensuous it turned ice into fire,
Seduced many young maidens to the tune of harp and lyre.

Innocence and goodness can't be bought or sold.
Lost it at the bell tower, but she never told.
Mama, it would have killed her! Papa, he wouldn't cared,
so she never told them She just never dared.

Sweet Poisoned Water

I was born in house of ill repute,
all Mama's clients thought I was cute.
They'd let me crawl up and sit on their laps
then Mama and them would take nice long naps.

I drank from the well of sweet, poisoned water,
but it never quenched my thirst as a daughter.
Oh Father, oh Father, I've loved you so well,
though just who you were I never could tell.

My brothers they came and visited me,
I looked in their eyes, and what did I see?
I saw my reflection, I saw my own life,
I knew that I never could be a man's wife.

I drank from the well of sweet, poisoned water,
How could you, oh Father, I was your own daughter!
Oh, brother, oh, brother, I've loved you so well,
Though just who I was I never could tell.

Unseasonal Rain

I don't want to hurt anymore.
Can't live with this lingering pain.
It's all come back to me tonight,
it must be the unseasonable rain.

It all happened so long ago,
it all happened so far away,
though I've tried, Lord knows that I've tried,
to forget what happened that day.

But it's all come back to me tonight,
it must be the unseasonable rain.
Lord, I don't want to hurt anymore,
just can't live with this lingering pain.

There must have been voices raised high,
there must have been cries of distress,
but I slept so soundly that night,
till the rain that awoke me, I guess.

The house was so quiet and still,
I could hear my heart beat in the gloom,
I gingerly walked down the hall
toward a light shining dim in their room.

My mother looked into my eyes,
said I hadn't seen what I just had.
But was that a gun in her hand,
the old gun that belonged to my dad?

I never saw Daddy again,
Daddy never came home anymore.
Now, had I seen blood covered sheets
and a man there dead on the floor?

So long was the time that'd gone by,
so much had gone on in between,
so hard I had tried to erase from my mind
things I shouldn't have seen.

And it all came back to me tonight,
must have been the unseasonable rain,
Lord, I just couldn't hurt anymore,
couldn't live with that lingering pain.

I begged mother to tell me the truth,
had I seen what I thought I saw?
She said I should give her more time
before I went to the law.

She went to the back of the house
and took Dad's old gun from the case.
And that shot ran out louder than truth,
than the truth Mother never could face.

Wooden Puzzle

You wanted much more than anyone could give you,
You wanted the sunlight to shine through the rain.
Had you told the truth I would have believed you,
But you just repeated the same old refrain:

Like a pressed wood nursery puzzle
left out in the pouring rain,
I'm unglued and I'm discolored!
It's no wonder I complain.

You sounded delirious. I thought you had fever.
You painted word pictures and tried to explain.
The glass was all shattered, all you had were pieces
Each one with a mark That had registered pain.
Elusive quicksilver ran down through your fingers,
Could have been diagnostic had it been contained.

Made in United States
Orlando, FL
15 July 2022

19840148R00150